Bedfordshire

40 Town & Country Walks

The authors and publisher have made every effort to ensure that the information in this publication is accurate, and accept no responsibility whatsoever for any loss, injury or inconvenience experienced by any person or persons whilst using this book.

published by
pocket mountains ltd
The Old Church, Annanside, Moffat,
Dumfries and Galloway DG10 9HB
www.pocketmountains.com

ISBN: 978-1-916739-20-8

A catalogue record for this book is available from the British Library

Contains Ordnance Survey data © Crown copyright and database 2026

Printed by J Thomson Colour Printers, Glasgow

MIX
Paper | Supporting
responsible forestry
FSC® C023105
FSC
www.fsc.org

Introduction

Bedfordshire is a gem of a county hidden in plain sight. Known to many only as part of a bedtime saying ('Up the wooden hill to Bedfordshire'), to others it's perceived simply as part of the urban expansion that is rapidly evolving between Oxford and Cambridge. Encircled by significant population centres, the county is crossed by hundreds of thousands daily yet is comparatively little known beyond its boundaries. Take a closer look, though, and this is an area that, despite ever-intensive development, retains a wealth of character and outdoor space and can still charm and delight.

A long and rich history combined with some outstanding attractions and areas of exquisite countryside help Bedfordshire retain its distinctive identity. This is one of England's smallest counties, yet here there are major sights such as Whipsnade Zoo and Woburn Abbey, not to mention the northeast end of the Chiltern Hills at Dunstable Downs and the Chilterns Area of Outstanding Natural Beauty, including the National Trust's Sharpenhoe and Sundon Hills. All of these feature in the walks in this guide.

History

As the Romans occupied lowland Britain, their expanded road network included Watling Street from Dover to Wroxeter. Along the stretch that we now know as the A5, they built several forts, including one – long since gone – at Dunstable, at the junction of Watling Street and the Icknield Way, Britain's oldest path. Roman Bedfordshire is visited in the first section of the Greensand Ridge Walk while part of the Icknield Way forms the Toddington route.

Most Bedfordshire towns were founded in the Middle Ages. Henry I built Bedford Castle overlooking the River Great Ouse in the 11th century, only for Henry III to tear it down again two centuries later. Leighton Buzzard and Ampthill markets developed and Bedford itself was granted a charter in 1166 and grew as a centre for the wool trade.

In the 16th to 19th centuries, successive monarchs granted baronies across the area, with a network of manors established, including much celebrated properties such as Wrest Park, Houghton House and, perhaps best known of all, Woburn Abbey. All three are included in walks in this guide.

The town of Luton developed in the 17th century thanks to a thriving hat-making industry, remnants of which are explored on the Luton walk. In more recent times, it became known for car manufacturing, especially Vauxhall Motors. Industrial development kicked in with the acquisition of Bedfordshire land by the London Brick Company. The local clay soils fuelled massive growth and by the 1930s the brickworks at Stewartby was the largest in the world, producing 500 million bricks a year, with 135 chimneys in Marston Vale. The brickworks closed in 2008, unable to meet UK limits for sulphur dioxide emissions, and today the chimneys have all gone.

During the Second World War, Bedfordshire played a key role, with RAF bases like Cardington and Thurleigh vital for training and air defence. Band leader Glen Miller was stationed in Bedford and his final flight before his disappearance over the Channel departed from here.

Huge post-war immigration to the region was driven by demand for bricks to help in the reconstruction of Britain's housing stock. The brick companies recruited from overseas and the local population surged with immigrants from Eastern Europe, Italy, India, Pakistan and the West Indies, helping to make the county the rich multi-cultural region it is today. Modern Bedfordshire is driven by sectors such as advanced engineering, logistics and agriculture. Luton remains a key economic hub, with London Luton Airport supporting trade and tourism. Cardington, once known for its airship heritage, is now a centre for film production at the historic Cardington Sheds.

Walking, weather and topography
A walk with a point of interest along the way is more rewarding than one without, so these routes generally have some sort of focus: a church, an historic connection or even just a bench with a fine view. Churches – usually with a handy bench for a pause in the churchyard – are a recurring theme, a reflection of the rural network of villages and hamlets.

The mild climate generally makes for easy walking, but winter can bring bitterly cold easterlies down the Bedford Levels while heatwaves are increasingly common in summer. The general rule is be prepared with a hat, scarf and waterproofs or summer hat and sunscreen.

The county is characterised by gentle hills, river valleys and a patchwork of arable and grazing fields, spinneys and woodland, heath remnants and wetlands. Look out for the stunning bee orchid, the county flower, particularly in areas of sandy soil during the summer (found at Stotfold and the meadows along the Great Ouse). On chalk grasslands, look for the dense pink flower spikes of pyramidal orchids and the pasque flower.

The Ouzel rises at the base of the Chiltern Hills and flows northwards to meet the River Great Ouse at Newport Pagnell. The Great Ouse meanders across the north of the county and through Bedford on its way to The Wash, joined in the east by the River Ivel. In southwest Bedfordshire, the Grand Union Canal passes through Leighton Buzzard. Note that after wet weather some routes may be extremely claggy underfoot or impassable due to flooding.

Travel

Travel round the region is generally easy, with a network of main road arteries – A1, M1, A6 and A5 – making non-rush hour driving quick. The East and West Coast Mainline railways both run through the region, and there are also stations at Luton and Bedford (with stops in between) and in the west between Bedford and Bletchley. Buses fan out from the main hubs of Bedford in the north and Luton in the south and generally offer good coverage to all the main towns and key villages.

About the guide

These 40 walks are a mix of classics and less explored routes that have been selected to reveal more unexpected parts. Distances range from 4km to 15km and timings are generally a maximum of three to four hours based on walking 3.5km-4km per hour, with extra time for steeper terrain. Not included in the times are refreshment breaks, wildlife spotting or stop-offs. In terms of chapter structure, divisions are based on a mix of

geographical features, major towns, transport routes and popularly accepted wisdom.

The illustrative maps included for each route are designed to be used in conjunction with the listed OS map detailed at the start of every walk (1:25,000). Generally, the level of detail they provide makes them most suitable for identifying key landscape features such as field boundaries or the various long-distance routes that cross the county, notably the Icknield Way Trail, John Bunyan Trail, Chiltern Way, North Beds Trail and Greensand Ridge Walk. Walking apps, paid for or free, such as Strava and OS, are also helpful for keeping on track.

On the majority of walks you may come across sheep or cattle; always keep dogs under control and on a lead, and avoid fields during lambing and calving seasons, which generally run March-May but can start earlier. Dogs should also be kept on a lead in sensitive wildlife habitats and where signs advise.

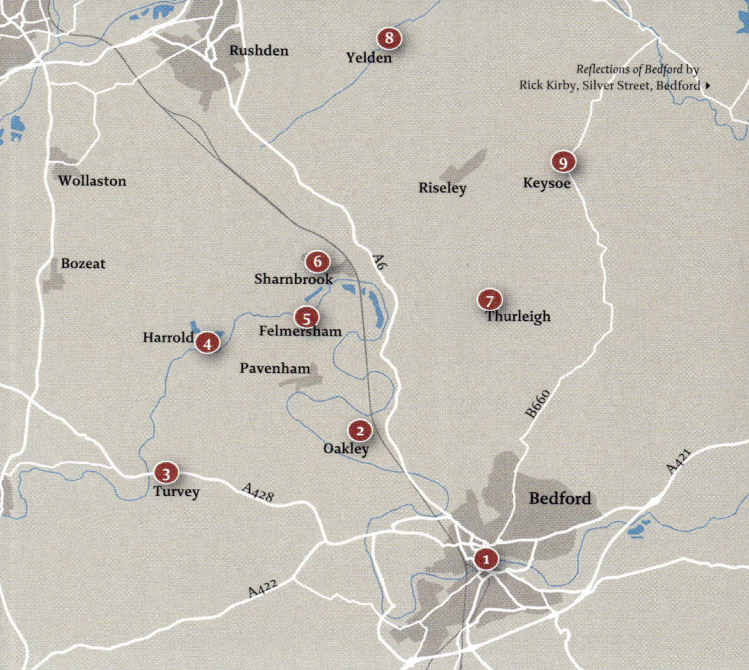

Rushden

Yelden **8**

Reflections of Bedford by
Rick Kirby, Silver Street, Bedford ▶

Wollaston

Riseley   Keysoe **9**

Bozeat

Sharnbrook **6**

A6

Harrold **4**   Felmersham **5**

Thurleigh **7**

Pavenham

B660

Oakley **2**

Turvey **3**

A428   A421

Bedford **1**

A422

The north of Bedfordshire makes up the quietest and most rural part of the county, an area which in look and feel is in parts reminiscent of the Cotswolds thanks to its mix of honey-coloured limestone, thatched cottages, church spires and gently rolling countryside. For those who are unfamiliar with this territory, the Bedfordshire Wolds come as something of a pleasant surprise.

Lively Bedford marks the southern boundary of this chapter, with a river and town trail that shows off the town to its best. It, too, offers surprises, not least the delightful Embankment along the river

and the town's mix of curious cultural attractions. The Great Ouse is a defining feature of much of this area, flowing generally west to east as it makes its way cross-country to empty into the Wash on the Norfolk coast. In its upper Bedfordshire reaches it winds lazily across the landscape in great arcs and loops, a haven for wildlife and a delightful accompaniment for walkers. Be warned, though: it can also be fickle and in wetter months is prone to flooding low-lying areas. The advice is to pay heed and not attempt sections of walks which may be affected.

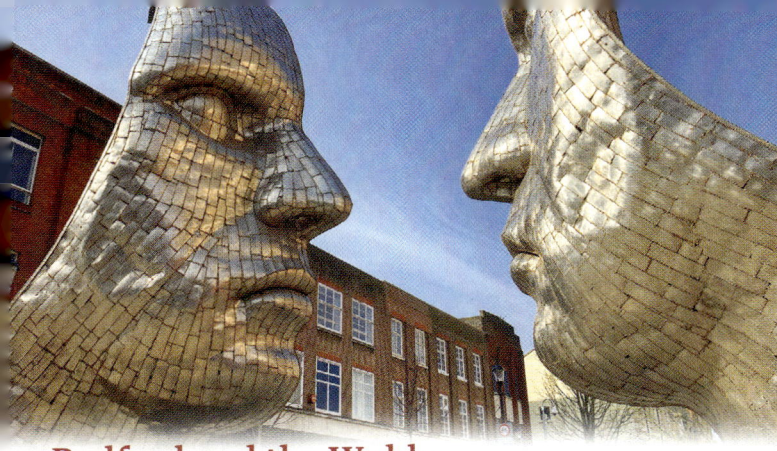

Bedford and the Wolds

1 **Bedford river and town trail**   8
Town, riverside and a leafy park are
combined in a choice of walks

2 **Oakley, Pavenham and Stevington**   10
This three-village ramble explores
riverside meadows, holy wells and a
windmill on the rise

3 **Turvey**   12
From Jonah to songbirds, elegant
grandeur to hedgerows brimming with
wildlife, this walk is full of surprises

4 **Harrold-Odell Country Park**   14
Rafts of ducks to an old lock-up, this is
a walk with plenty of village character

5 **Felmersham and Radwell**   16
This varied route linking river
meadows and village greens also takes
in one of the county's finest churches

6 **Sharnbrook**   18
From swan-upping to wildfowl
watching, this short walk blends
village heritage with watery habitats

7 **Thurleigh**   20
Wartime history, motorsports and
gentle countryside offer an intriguing
mix of traditional and modern in and
around this pretty village

8 **Yelden, Upper Dean
and Melchbourne**   22
Explore the far-flung parishes
where motte and manor still shape
the landscape

9 **Keysoe**   24
A former lace-making village known
today for its equestrian centre, this
peaceful parish was once a hotbed of
religious dissent

Bedford river and town trail

Distance 3.5km or 8km for longer route
Time 1 hour/2 hours 30 **Terrain** pavement
and footpaths **Map** OS Explorer 208
Access buses to Bedford from surrounding
villages and towns; trains to Bedford from
London, Luton, and Bletchley

**Celebrities, famous architects and
religious non-conformists have all left
their mark on the county town. Revel in
its history and character, wander by the
River Great Ouse and retreat to its leafy
gardens in this enlightening town trail.**

From the Mill Meadows riverside car
park cross the footbridge and turn left,
passing the bandstand and heading for
the town centre. Enjoy the fine view of the
Swan Hotel on the north bank as you
follow the river, crossing several small
bridges, before ducking underneath the
elegant Georgian Town Bridge.

At the next footbridge cross the river
and continue diagonally right over
Riverside Square to pass between the
Old Town Hall and Cowper Building to
St Paul's Square. Turn right and, at the
pedestrian crossing, cross to the centre for
an anti-clockwise stroll around the square.
Alfred Gilbert, of Piccadilly Circus *Eros*
fame, designed the statue of prison
reformer John Howard, who was the
High Sherriff of Bedfordshire in the 18th
century. A little further round the square
is the Corn Exchange of 1874, which in
its time has welcomed many stars,
including Bing Crosby and Marlene
Dietrich. At the centre is St Paul's Church,
possibly founded as early as the 8th
century, although today's building dates
mainly from the 15th century.

Cross at the pedestrian crossing to
Harpur Street, pass the eye-catching

◀ River Great Ouse, Bedford

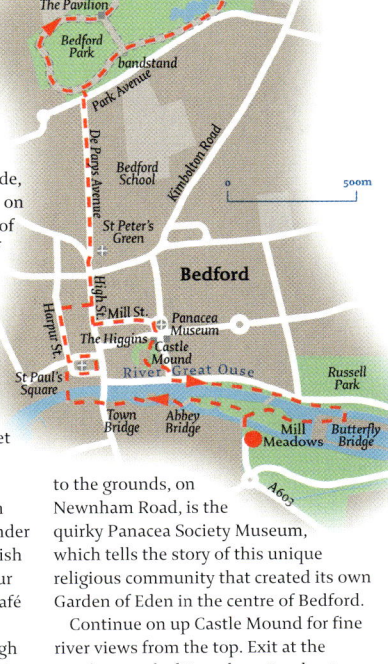

Harpur Centre (once Bedford Modern School), the eastern façade of which was designed by Edward Blore, best known for his completion of Buckingham Palace. Carry on straight ahead and just after Silver Street turn right into the Edwardian shopping arcade, with its mix of independent shops, and on exiting at the far side go left to the end of the High Street and the statue of one of Bedford's most famous sons, religious reformer John Bunyan, on St Peter's Green. St Peter's Church in the centre of the green has some of the town's oldest architectural remains, including two Saxon monoliths.

For a shorter walk, retrace your steps back down the High Street to Mill Street and pick up the route from there (see below). For a longer walk, and to visit Bedford Park, continue ahead and then right along De Parys Avenue for just under 1km. The park is grade II listed by English Heritage and dates from 1888. Take your pick of routes around the bandstand, café and duck pond.

Retrace your steps back down the High Street, turning left onto Mill Street, at the far end of which, in Bedford's Cultural Quarter, stands the Bunyan Meeting Church and Museum, both worth a visit for an insight into Bunyan's life. Facing St Cuthbert's Church on the roundabout, head right and enter the grounds of The Higgins art/museum hub (also worth a visit). Just over the road from the entrance

to the grounds, on Newnham Road, is the quirky Panacea Society Museum, which tells the story of this unique religious community that created its own Garden of Eden in the centre of Bedford.

Continue on up Castle Mound for fine river views from the top. Exit at the southern end of Newnham Road onto The Embankment. Turn left along the waterside for around 750m, past the gardens and the elegant suspension bridge. Cross the river on the Butterfly Bridge and turn right to wander past the boating lake and the Archimedean Screw Turbine back to the bandstand and car park.

9

Oakley, Pavenham and Stevington

Distance 13km **Time** 3 hours
Terrain footpath, meadows and road
verges **Map** OS Explorer 208
Access buses to Oakley from Bedford
and Rushden

**Visit three villages and walk a section
of the Ouse Valley Way and John Bunyan
Trail on this sweeping meander of the
Great Ouse.**

Start at St Mary's Church in Oakley
(parking available), with its interesting
singlehanded clock from around 1620.
Turn right out of the car park and at the
T-junction go left along Church Lane for
500m and then right onto the High Street.
This part of the village was influenced by
the Dukes of Bedford's past stewardship:
look out for the inscriptions of ducal
coronet, 'B' and year of construction on
many of the cottage gables.

At the crossroads go left, heading out of
the village, and into Linch Furlong
community nature reserve on the right.
Aim for the footpath in the bottom left
corner and, once back at the road, turn
right over the river and continue carefully
along the road. After about 500m, take the
footpath on the left, initially following the
hedgerow along the field and then
woodland. Look out for the distinctive
banded demoiselle damselflies in summer.

At the 'no entry' gate go right and stay
with the path winding along the wood and
field edge into the trees and then along a
broad track. At the farm go through the
kissing gate and another gate on the right,
then up to the road. Turn left, then in
180m right onto another footpath running
along the back of the houses. At the road
go right and then left onto another
footpath leading to Pavenham's delightful
12th- to 13th-century St Peter's Church.

Turn left down the road into the village,

◀ High Street, Pavenham

then right at the T-junction, passing the pretty limestone cottages, rambling roses and the inviting Cock pub along the High Street. Go left down Mill Lane and on through the kissing gate signed 'Ouse Valley Way'. The path soon wends through attractive riverside meadows, rich in summer flowers and orchids, but does become indistinct at times, particularly under high season growth, and can also be boggy. Make your way along to a metal gate and footbridge close to the river after about 1km.

Gradually head away from the river and along the back of a wood (look out for the waymarker post). Pass through a few kissing gates, cross another meadow and, at the end of the woodland, go through the kissing gate onto the main path following the wood edge and hedgerow. The path does a sharp right, now offering fine views over the Great Ouse valley to the left.

Stay with this path as it passes St Mary's Holy Well and soon comes to St Mary the Virgin Church, finely situated overlooking the river. Follow the road down past the lovely gardens and cottages to reach the

crossroads with its 13th-century cross. (The keys may be available from either of the pubs if you wish to enter the windmill.)

Go left, following the road out of the village and, just after the pavement runs out, turn right onto Windmill Lane. Continue on the footpath to the left, but first pop up to explore the timber post windmill, built around 1770. At the fingerpost take the bridleway left to the road, turn left and then quickly right onto a footpath leading down to the river.

Follow the riverside path for about 1km to the road, go left over Oakley Bridge and right into the meadow with the Ouse Valley Walk sign back to the church and car park.

Turvey

Distance 11.5km **Time** 3 hours
Terrain footpaths, parkland, pavements
and quiet lanes **Map** OS Explorer 208
Access buses to Turvey from Bedford
and Northampton

**This picturesque walk blends the tranquil
River Great Ouse with rolling countryside
and Turvey's rich heritage. Stroll past
elegant limestone cottages, spot herons
and egrets along the riverbank, and watch
for muntjac deer on a woodland path.**

Crossing from Buckinghamshire into
Bedfordshire, begin at the lay-by next to
historic Turvey Bridge – believed to be
the oldest bridged crossing of the River
Great Ouse, first recorded in 1140. Pass
the former Turvey Mill where you may
spot two statues on the riverbank – Jonah,
brought from Ashridge House in 1844,
and his mysterious companion, who
arrived in 1953.

Continue into Turvey village, passing
the Three Fyshes pub before turning right
at the Festival of Britain 1951 village sign
onto Newton Lane. Many of the honey-
coloured limestone buildings here owe
their character to the 19th-century Higgins
family, erstwhile owners of Turvey Abbey,
who undertook widespread improvements
to benefit their tenants.

After about 100m, cross the road and
take the footpath on the left opposite
Nell's Well – one of several water pumps
once relied upon by villagers before mains
water arrived in the 1950s. Keep to the left-
hand path across the grazing paddock,
then quickly cross to the right-hand one to
enter the woodland. Follow the path
through a kissing gate, then cross the
driveway and step into Turvey Abbey
Park. Pass the small castellated tower built
in 1829 as a garden house for John Higgins
and continue across the parkland. This

Turvey

◀ Castellated garden house
in Turvey Abbey Park

landscape has been defined
by the 17th-century Turvey
Abbey and its wider estate.
Despite its name, the abbey
didn't have a monastic role
until 1980 when it was bought by
a Benedictine Order from Cockfosters
in North London.

Leaving the park through a kissing gate,
enter the woods and turn right at a
T-junction near a footbridge, soon
emerging to follow the woodland edge
for roughly 600m. After crossing the
railway bridge, the bridleway meanders
alongside hedgerows and field boundaries,
offering a chance to spot lapwings and
yellowhammers all year round. This
tranquil landscape is a patchwork of arable
farmland, wooded spinneys and distant
farmhouses connected by a traditional
network of hedgerows.

Continue along the track with hedgerow
on both sides for around 800m until you
reach a gap with a waymarker post, where
you turn right onto another bridleway.
After approximately 1.5km, turn right at
the bridleway fork and then right again at
the next T-junction, soon joining a quiet
country road.

Follow the road, enjoying the mass of
cowslips if visiting in spring. Turn right at
the T-junction and then immediately take
the waymarked bridleway on the right.
Continue ahead for almost 2km along
hedgerows and woodland edges, taking in
the sweeping countryside views and a

final climb up to Church's Cottage.

Turn left along the lane, cross the
railway bridge and, just before another
cottage, turn right onto the footpath.
Follow the woodland edge with views of
Turvey village ahead. On meeting the
outbound route, turn left back to the
village sign and A428. Before returning to
the starting point, cross the road to take a
detour up the High Street and explore
Turvey's elegant centre with its pretty
cottages, butcher's shop, pub, store and
Turvey House and Gardens (check website
for open days), finishing at the fine setting
of All Saints Church.

Harrold-Odell Country Park

Distance 7km **Time** 1 hour 30
Terrain footpaths and pavement
Map OS Explorer 208 **Access** buses to
Harrold from Bedford

The villages of Harrold and Odell lie at opposite ends of a broad bend of the River Great Ouse. In between them, the 58ha Harrold-Odell Country Park incorporates washed-out gravel pits last used in the 1980s that have been filled to create a haven for wildlife in Grebe Lake and the smaller Kingfisher Water. This walk explores the country park before returning through pretty Harrold.

From the car park for the country park, take the signposted River Walk path. Follow the southern side of Kingfisher Water before curving left to wander up the meadows for around 1km along the bank of the Great Ouse. The river meanders

lazily in summer, its banks lined by willows, but becomes more forceful in autumn and winter, when the meadow can flood. On a hill to the right stands the deconsecrated 12th-century Chellington Church, while ahead the top of the church tower at Odell appears above the trees. Listen out for green woodpecker and the scratchy song of sedge warbler, and look out for lapwing; in summer you are likely to see the metallic blue of banded demoiselle damselflies.

Keep to the path where it veers away from the river, go through a kissing gate and carry on ahead. Pass Silt Lake on the left and, at a junction, cross the main Odell path to follow the signposted Grebe Lake Walk. At the next path junction, keep ahead with the lake to your left, passing a number of named fishing pegs. Cross a wooden bridge and pass a bird hide, then

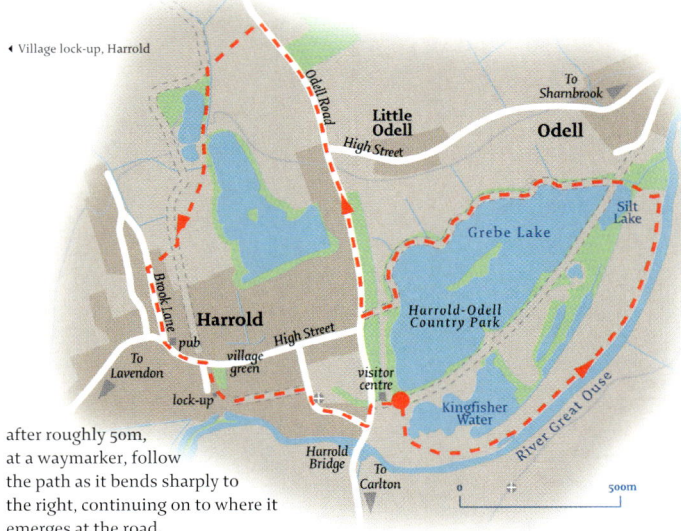

◀ Village lock-up, Harrold

after roughly 50m,
at a waymarker, follow
the path as it bends sharply to
the right, continuing on to where it
emerges at the road.

On reaching the road, go right for 1km, passing Little Odell High Street and, as the road reaches the top of the rise, take the signposted path to the left.

To follow the designated path, cross straight over the field (look for the waymarker directly opposite), then go left along the fenceline. In the corner of the field, go through a kissing gate and follow the path. After the next kissing gate continue ahead across the field with the hedgerow on your right. Cross a stile and follow the track as it skirts the edge of the field round to the left.

Look out for a signpost, at which go right in the direction of Brook Lane. On reaching the lane, go left to wander through Harrold, a village built largely on the leather industry which at one point had six leather factories. Follow the road past a row of quaint cottages and on reaching the Oakley Arms pub at the main road, go left.

The village green is lined by pretty cottages. Here, too, stands the original 18th-century buttermarket and 19th-century village lock-up. Cut across the green diagonally, passing the lock-up, and take the path between the houses. Head right to skirt St Peter's Church and then left to reach the main road, at which go left again to return to the start.

Felmersham and Radwell

Distance 13km **Time** 3 hours
Terrain footpaths, grassland, pavements and country lanes **Map** OS Explorer 208
Access buses to Felmersham from Bedford and Kettering

With its magnificently arcaded west front, Felmersham's 13th-century church is one of the finest in the county and makes a striking end to this varied walk that encompasses past industry, nature and history. Follow winding trails through quiet countryside and quaint villages, cross historic river bridges and pass through meadows alive with summer butterflies.

Note: sections flood after heavy rain, livestock may be present and some paths can be overgrown in summer.

From the car park at the Wildlife Trust's Felmersham Gravel Pits SSSI, cross the road and keep ahead on the main reserve path along the side of the former gravel pits. Gravel was extracted during the Second World War to build the nearby airfields, but today this once industrial site is a lush watery haven for wildlife and, with some 18 breeding species, one of the best places for dragonflies and damselflies in the county. Exit the reserve via the far kissing gate and turn right, then left at the path T-junction, with a view of Sharnbrook spire and windmill. Turn right at the waymarker and continue on over a succession of bridges across the Pinchmill Islands – named after a long-gone mill – in the Great Ouse.

Continue ahead for roughly 1.3km along a section that can be overgrown to Radwell village. Along the way, cross Brook Farm farmyard (take the path at the end of the yard with the stile), continue along a field edge and over a wildflower meadow – look out for oxeye daisies and common blue butterflies in summer – then carry on along the hedgerow and through a couple of kissing gates near the houses, before turning right at the track.

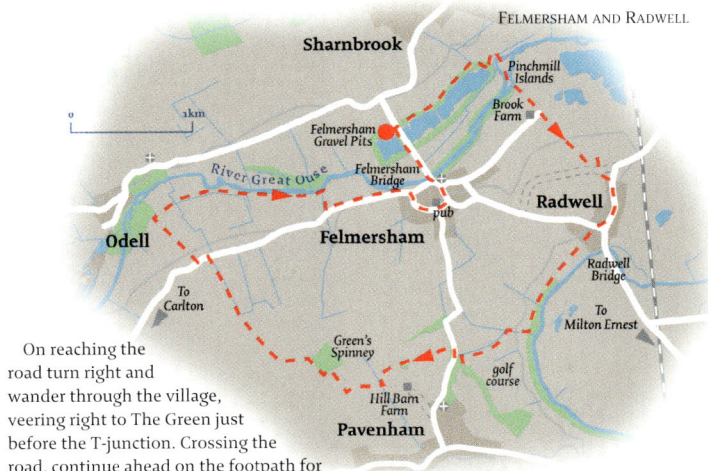

Sharnbrook

Pinchmill
Islands

Brook
Farm

Felmersham
Gravel Pits

Felmersham
Bridge

River Great Ouse

pub

Radwell

Odell

Felmersham

Radwell
Bridge

To
Carlton

To
Milton Ernest

Green's
Spinney

golf
course

Hill Barn
Farm

Pavenham

On reaching the road turn right and wander through the village, veering right to The Green just before the T-junction. Crossing the road, continue ahead on the footpath for roughly 1km to the edge of the golf course. At the waymarker post turn right onto the initially clear footpath along the hedgerow and at the open fairways cross ahead, moving slightly left to keep the ditch and hedge on your right. Cross the hard-surface golf track to curve left and go along the footpath on the right, through the woods, to the road.

Turn right, then left after roughly 100m along the bridleway crossing fields. Keep with this route as it crosses this higher plateau with views all around and a glimpse of Stevington Windmill to the left. At the copse keep ahead on the main path (maps show the path crossing the field), go left at the hedge, then right and stay with the bridleway to a metal gate and waymarker post. Turn right along the footpath, skirt the southwest edge of Green's Spinney, continue along the field edge and hedgerow and then go on up to Carlton Road. In summer listen out for skylark, yellowhammer and cuckoo.

Go left for around 120m, then right at the bridleway up the field edge, turning right at the footpath waymarker post. The footpath initially follows a hedgerow and runs over grassland before reaching a particularly lovely stretch of riverside.

Cross the footbridge, turn immediately right and at the road turn left to carefully walk along the verge for roughly 700m. Upon entering Felmersham, take Grange Road on the right, follow this past The Sun Inn and at the T-junction turn left downhill into the heart of the village with its honey-coloured limestone cottages, Tithe Barn and historic church.

Continue along the road to cross the distinctive five-arched bridge, beyond which go left through the kissing gate into the nature reserve and along the right-hand path back to the start.

◀ River bridge at Felmersham

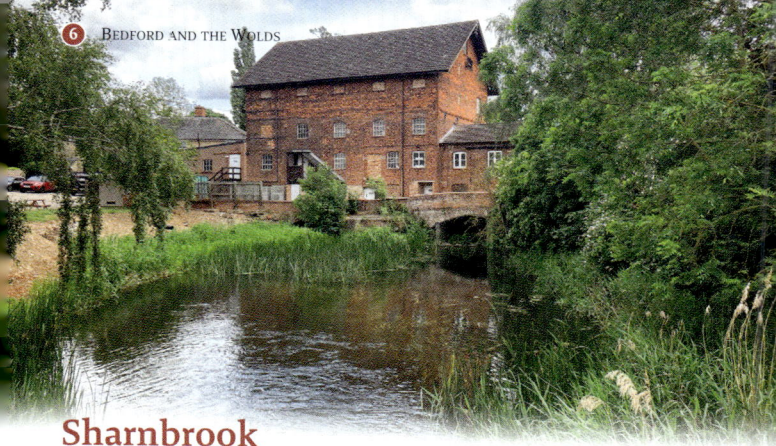

Sharnbrook

Distance 6.5km **Time** 2 hours
Terrain footpaths, grassland, pavements
and quiet lanes **Map** OS Explorer 208
Access buses to Sharnbrook from Bedford
and Kettering

**Explore Sharnbrook and its environs on
this short walk or combine it with the
Felmersham route for a longer trail. Either
way, scenic views, charming cottages and
wildlife-rich wetlands make for an
appealing mix.**

Start from Sharnbrook's oldest surviving
building, St Peter's Church, first recorded
in about 1155. Leave the churchyard, turn
left and head into the village centre and
the pretty streets leading off from the
small green, surrounded by honey-
coloured limestone cottages, shops and a
café. Look out for the old lion head
standpipe installed in the 1930s as part of a
scheme to provide water to all parishes.

At the T-junction turn right down the
High Street and pass the Swan with Two
Nicks pub. Its unusual name honours the
swan-upping census on the Thames, in
which swans were traditionally 'marked'
one nick for the Dyers and two for the
Vintners who, through Royal Charter,
shared in the Sovereign's ownership.

A little further on, note the plaque at
the primary school stating this was the
county's first 'Board' school, created after
the 1870 Education Act and replacing
church schools with secular, publicly
funded education.

Pass the rather grand former police
station, following the road's sharp curve
to the left, and carry on up the gradual
incline of Kennel Hill, staying ahead on
Mill Road as it veers right at the road
junction. Continue under the railway
bridges and after roughly 500m turn right
at the bridleway down to Sharnbrook
Mill Theatre. A mill is recorded here in
the Domesday Book of 1086 and milling

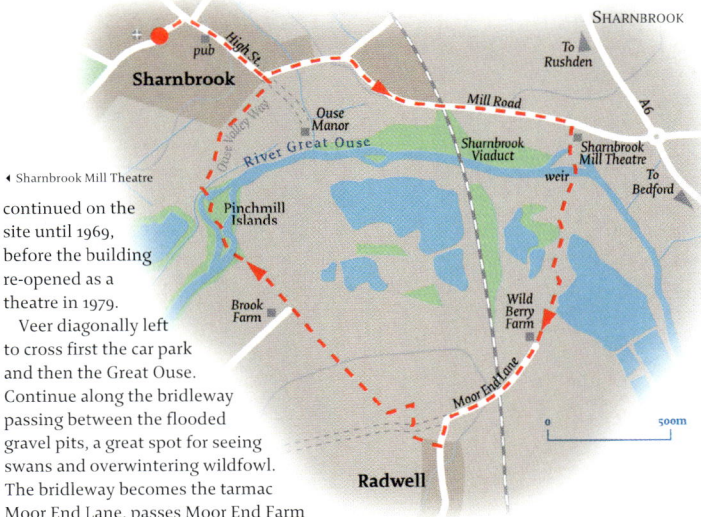

To Rushden

To Bedford

Sharnbrook

pub

High St

Ouse Valley Way

Ouse Manor

River Great Ouse

Mill Road

Sharnbrook Viaduct

Sharnbrook Mill Theatre

weir

A6

Pinchmill Islands

Brook Farm

Wild Berry Farm

Moor End Lane

Radwell

0   500m

◀ Sharnbrook Mill Theatre

continued on the site until 1969, before the building re-opened as a theatre in 1979.

Veer diagonally left to cross first the car park and then the Great Ouse. Continue along the bridleway passing between the flooded gravel pits, a great spot for seeing swans and overwintering wildfowl. The bridleway becomes the tarmac Moor End Lane, passes Moor End Farm (also known as Wild Berry Farm), continues over the railway and takes a sharp left into Radwell.

To explore the village, continue ahead; otherwise, immediately after the first house on the right (Five Elms), follow the track on the right for roughly 1.3km to Pinchmill Islands at the Great Ouse. To get there, cross a lane and after almost 100m go left then right through a couple of kissing gates. Cross over a wildflower meadow and continue straight across the Brook Farm farmyard, looking out for – and going through – a kissing gate and then along the fenced path ahead, soon passing a caravan park to reach the river. This final stretch can be overgrown with stinging nettles in spring and summer, when it is also filled with dragonflies and beautiful banded demoiselle damselflies.

Cross a succession of bridges over the Great Ouse at Pinchmill Islands, so-named after a mill which once stood here and may have belonged to a small manor or farm named Pynche. This is an idyllic spot to linger and enjoy the watery channels, lush vegetation and dreamy weeping willow. The site also offers plenty of wildlife-watching opportunities with mallard ducks, heron, egret and, if very lucky, otter to be spied.

Once across the river and through the metal gate, turn right onto the bridleway. (This is also the point at which to link with the Felmersham walk.)

Crossing the field, stay ahead on the bridleway, pass the sail-less windmill and, at the road, turn left to rejoin the outbound route and retrace your steps to St Peter's Church.

Thurleigh

Distance 6km **Time** 1 hour 30
Terrain footpath, fields and quiet lanes
Map OS Explorer 208 **Access** buses to
Thurleigh from Bedford and Kimbolton

Standing on a 77m-high plateau, pretty
Thurleigh (pronounced *Thur-lie*) was the
site of a Norman castle, although the spot
was also occupied in the Iron Age, and by
Romans and Saxons. Between 1946 and
1994 it was the location of Royal Aircraft
Establishment (RAE) Bedford, a research
site for aircraft experimental work,
including the intriguing Rolls-Royce
Flying Bedstead, an early vertical take-off
and landing aircraft.

   This gentle walk starts from the village
hall in the High Street, where limited
parking is available (you can also park on
the street). With your back to the hall, go
right along the street and downhill,
passing the war memorial where an

American flag is flown alongside a Union
flag, commemorating the 306th
Bombardment Group that was stationed
here from the US in 1942. Carry on past
St Peter's Church with its Norman tower,
then take the signposted public footpath to
the left along the bottom of the churchyard,
soon emerging into a field. Continue ahead
and, where the path splits, go on to a pond
and then carry on for a further 1km with a
ditch on your right, passing two paths
going off to the right.

   Just after two lines of trees, cross the
sleeper bridge over the ditch and continue
straight ahead for almost 500m, at the end
of which follow the path around to the
right to – and through – a field gate and
onwards up to the road.

   Cross over carefully and carry on straight
ahead, ignoring paths off to the left. Climb
two waymarked stiles in quick succession
and at the far side of the next field carry on

◀ War memorial, Thurleigh

gently uphill to the right. Cross another two stiles at a ditch and keep ahead with the fenceline still on your left. At the top of the field, climb the stile and go straight ahead across a tarmac lane and a patch of grass to reach the main road.

Cross the road carefully and walk just over 500m up the driveway signposted Blackburn Hall Farm. At a gate that prevents access to the business premises ahead, continue to the right around the edge of the buildings and into a field on the far side, at which point turn right up the field towards the road. About halfway up, the right of way goes left across the field and then right up to the road. However, if the field is planted with crops, there may also be a continuous path line straight up. Beyond the field off to the left lies the huge expanse of the former Thurleigh airfield, the northern section of which is the location of both Thurleigh Museum and Bedford Autodrome, designed from scratch by former Formula 1 driver Jonathan Palmer.

Turn right along the road and follow it back into Thurleigh, with a view to the right of sail-less Thurleigh Windmill, now part of a private house. Pass on the left, sitting below street level, some old thatched 'Squatters' Cottages', so-called because they were originally built – usually very quickly – as basic dwellings by the homeless poor in the mistaken belief that so long as a building could be erected and have a fire lit and smoke issuing from the chimney within a day, it would be legally permissible.

At the junction with the High Street, turn left uphill to return to the village hall.

Yelden, Upper Dean and Melchbourne

Distance 14km **Time** 3 hours 30
Terrain footpaths, fields and quiet lanes
Maps OS Explorer 224 and 225
Access infrequent buses to Yelden from
Bedford and Rushden, and to Upper Dean
from Bedford and Kimbolton

Explore the county's charming northern
reaches of Yelden, Shelton, Upper Dean
and Melchbourne, each nestled in
undulating countryside and boasting
a rich history, including dramatic
earthworks, manor houses and a windmill.

Turn left out of Yelden village hall car
park, passing St Mary's Church with its
octagonal broach spire. Turn right at
Church Lane, left at High Street and then
first left to follow the Three Shires Way
out of the village. This broad track cuts
across open countryside, a place of big
skies with red kite, buzzard and, in winter,
flocks of fieldfare. Stay on the signed
byway for roughly 1.5km to a Three Shires
Way fingerpost and take the small lane
into the hamlet of Shelton, part of the
county's most northerly parish.

Entering Shelton, take the footpath
on the right through the farmyard (or
alternatively go on a few extra paces
for a quick look at 12th-century St Mary's
Church). Follow the path along the barn
side, over a little bridge on the River Till,
up a slight incline and then across a
couple of fields to the windmill of 1850
on Oakley Hill.

Take a quick right, then left around the
windmill. Follow the footpath down
through a hedgerow tunnel, over a
wooden bridge and, just before Wynstead
Barn, continue on the rerouted footpath
on the left, which quickly goes right,
crossing over the driveway, and carries on
down to the road. Turn right and
follow the road to Church Lane
where you go left to reach the
13th-century All Hallows
Church, with its grotesque
heads and gargoyles.

Shelton

Oakley Hill

windmill

Three Shires Way

pub

Dean Lodge

Upper Dean

Top Farm

Yelden

village hall

earthworks

Grange Farm

To Rushden

Crowfield Farm

Vicarage Farm

pub

Barton's Spinney

Melchbourne

0   1km

From the church, head along the High Street and turn right at the T-junction to follow the road out of the village (no pavement), passing the Three Compasses pub. At the 40mph sign, take the tarmac bridleway on the right up through Dean Lodge. Turn left at the end of the buildings along the broad track. When it curves right on the approach to Grange Farm, take the path on the left and walk two sides of the field before going left down the main driveway.

Cross straight over the main road, pass St Johns Arms pub, then take Park Road into Melchbourne village, with views over to Melchbourne House and Park. After the long row of handsome thatched cottages, St Mary Magdalene Church comes into view, a rare example of a rural church with a Georgian interior. If not visiting the church, take the bridleway on the right and go immediately right again on the footpath.

At the road, cross over onto another footpath winding away from the village, around some paddocks and then around the outer edges of Barton's Spinney. Keep to the right of the telegraph pole, cross the stream and at the waymarker post follow the track to the left and then right up to Crowfield Farm. Keep ahead to cross the field after the farm, turn right at the bridleway along the field edge, then left at the footpath, heading back towards Yelden. The path crosses a field and follows the hedge along the field edge; you then climb over a stile and head diagonally towards the church, passing to the left of the impressive Yielden (note the interchangeable village spelling) Castle motte and bailey. Described as one of the finest archaeological monuments in the county, it was first recorded in 1173 as the stronghold of the Trailly family.

Turn right at the road and then left up Spring Lane to return to the start.

◀ Upper Dean Windmill on Oakley Hill

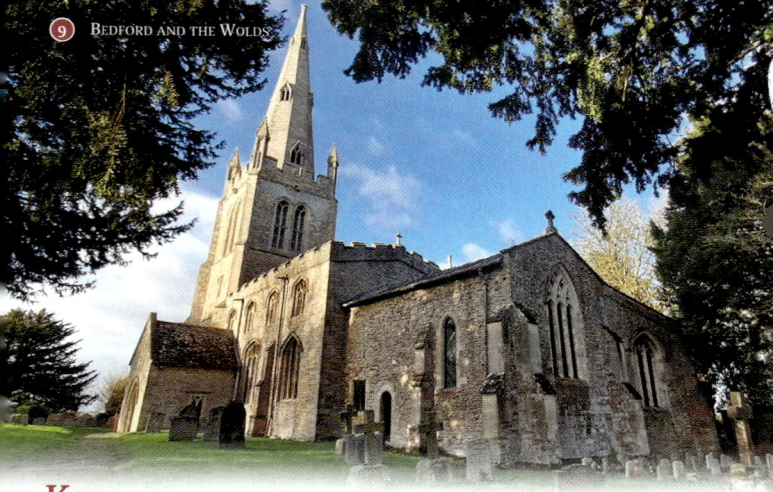

Keysoe

Distance 7km **Time** 1 hour 30
Terrain field paths, bridleways and
country lane **Map** OS Explorer 225
Access buses from Bedford to Keysoe,
then pick up the route at St Mary's Church

In times past the village of Keysoe was
largely ignored by successive Lords of the
Manor and became something of a centre
for dissenters, soon attracting the
attention of an itinerant preacher from
Elstow, John Bunyan. He came here to be
amongst like-minded non-conformists and
on one occasion was arrested with several
local men while preaching outdoors.

Start at the southwestern tip of
Keysoepark Wood (limited parking in a
lay-by at the corner of the wood), roughly
3km along Riseley Road from Brook End,
the northern section of Keysoe village. The
wood itself is private, so for the first leg go
immediately left across a bridge over a
ditch and follow the edge of the wood (on
your right) up the right-hand side of a field
for 500m. At a waymarker for the North
Bedfordshire Heritage Trail, go right
across a ditch and then left along the edge
of a field, with a hedge on your left. Look
out for the prominent spire of St Mary's
Church off to the east, a focal point for
much of this walk.

Follow the line of the hedge for just
over 1km, ignoring a path joining from the
left and passing through gaps at the end
of three hedgerows to reach the northern
corner of a field, where a bridleway joins
from the left. In winter it can be muddy
underfoot. Turn right here for a short
stretch and, after crossing a ditch at a
junction with a bridleway, continue to the

◀ St Mary's Church, Keysoe

right with a ditch and hedge on your right and the spire of St Mary's Church on the hill ahead.

On reaching a track, keep ahead into the next field, at which point bear slightly left (left of the spire in the distance) to cross the field, aiming for the houses and a yellow bridleway marker. Continue down a narrow bridleway between trees, cross over Keysoe Brook and emerge on the Riseley road. Turn right along the road and then shortly after take the footpath uphill to the left to St Mary's Church. Look for the plaque on the wall which commemorates William Dickins, a stonemason who in 1718 fell from the tower and somehow survived.

Exiting the churchyard to the road, go

right for 200m and, just past Vicarage Farm, take the bridleway on the right down to the road, at which go straight across and through a kissing gate. Head left along the hedgeline and then follow the path as it bears right across the field to a yellow waymarker. Continue on over the next field and through a gap in the hedge at a telegraph pole. Turn right here and walk up the entrance drive to Park Farm, up to the big brick-built sheds. Go through the kissing gate on the left and cross the field diagonally to the right to a kissing gate in the far corner. There may be livestock here.

Carry on ahead across the next field to the eastern corner of Keysoepark Wood. Keeping the wood on your right, follow the edge back to the start, nipping out to the road through a gap in the hedge at the southwest corner.

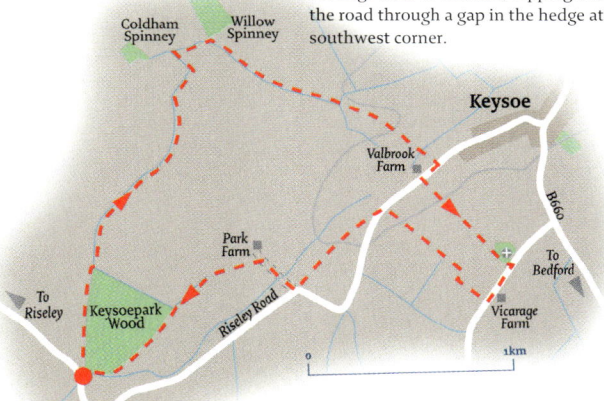

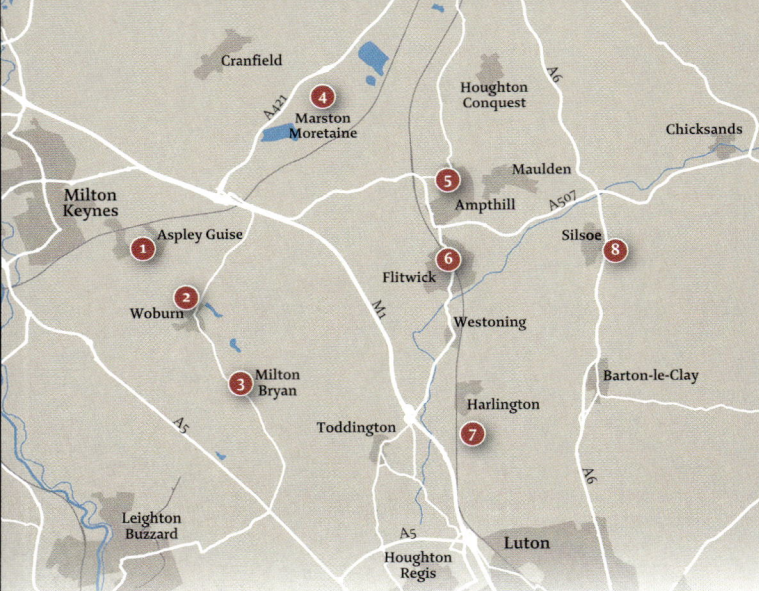

Cranfield

Houghton
Conquest

4 Marston
Moreitane

A421

A6

Chicksands

5 Maulden

Milton
Keynes

Aspley Guise

1

Ampthill

A507

Silsoe

8

6

Flitwick

2 Woburn

M1

Westoning

Barton-le-Clay

3 Milton
Bryan

A5

Harlington

7

Toddington

A6

Leighton
Buzzard

A5

Houghton
Regis

Luton

West Bedfordshire offers a rich blend of stately heritage and varied landscapes. This chapter explores an area that feels cultivated yet quietly wild – from the planned grandeur of Woburn Abbey and Ampthill Great Park to the open Sundon Hills' chalky ridges and wet Flitwick Moor.

Georgian Woburn and Ampthill offer charm and character. Woburn, with its elegant streets, owes much to the Dukes of Bedford, whose seat at Woburn Abbey remains a centrepiece. Ampthill is on a more intimate scale: its parkland was once the setting for royal drama, with Katherine of Aragon held here during her separation from Henry VIII.

The geology underfoot is as varied as the history above it. Sandy and clay soils dominate the lower ground, giving way to the chalk escarpments. These shifts support a diversity of habitats, including the county's largest wetland, remnant heathland and rare chalk grassland flora.

Silsoe adds another layer of grandeur with Wrest Park, once home to the de Grey family. Its fine gardens, Baroque architecture and nearby mausoleum, in Flitton, make it a visitor highlight. Spiritual heritage is woven through the area's history in the influence of John Bunyan, non-conformist preacher and author of *The Pilgrim's Progress*.

Katherine's Cross, Ampthill Great Park ▶

West Bedfordshire

1 **Aspley Guise
and Husborne Crawley** 28
A short circuit with woodland shade,
sculptural surprises and a dash of
Bedford Estate history

2 **Woburn** 30
Magnificent Woburn Abbey forms the
centrepiece of this delightful ramble.
Despite its popularity, the crowds are
soon left behind

3 **Milton Bryan and Eversholt** 32
A walk of quiet lanes, oak collection,
secret wartime broadcasts and a couple
of pubs worth pausing for

4 **Marston Moretaine and Lidlington** 34
Where once stood mighty brick pits,
today explore a new woodland in the
heart of Marston Vale

5 **Ampthill** 36
Enjoy fine Georgian architecture, a
romantic hilltop ruin and a Spanish-
inspired promenade

6 **Flitwick and Flitton Moors** 38
Take a wander through a nationally
important SSSI, home to a range of
threatened species

7 **Sundon Hills
and Sharpenhoe Clappers** 40
Blow away the cobwebs on this classic
Chilterns walk with rare orchids,
soaring red kites and Iron Age history

8 **Silsoe and Higham Gobion** 42
From a grand château to sleepy
hamlets, this walk offers grandeur
and quiet charm in equal measure

Aspley Guise and Husborne Crawley

Distance 7.5km **Time** 2 hours
Terrain footpaths, pavements and quiet
lanes **Map** OS Explorer 192
Access buses to Aspley Guise from
Woburn, Milton Keynes, Flitwick and
Leighton Buzzard; trains to Aspley Guise
from Bletchley and Bedford

In 1857, local doctor James Williams
proclaimed Aspley Guise to be on a
par with the most popular health resorts
of the day, igniting a flurry of
entrepreneurial building activity that
helped to make the village the elegant
place it is now. This gentle walk takes in
the 'healing air', lush woodland and open
heath of the surrounding area.

Starting in The Square, beside the
timber pavilion and village sign, head up
the gentle incline of West Hill, with the
Moore Place Hotel on your left. The name
Aspley Guise is thought to stem from
Aspen-Leigh (a clearing in aspen woods)
and from the de Guise family, notable
landowners in Tudor times – most
famously Mary de Guise, mother of Mary,
Queen of Scots.

As the road curves gently right, cross
over and follow narrow Wood Lane. At the
T-junction, continue ahead on the
bridleway into the woods. Turn left at the
footpath marker and pass through
fragments of ancient broadleaf woodland,
now mixed with conifers planted for
timber. Watch for common lizards basking
on the warmer open ground.

Continue straight on at the first marker
and go left at the second, looking out for
fancifully-named Mermaid's Pond to your
right. Follow the path to exit the
woodland, heading straight across the
road and up towards Birchmoor Farm.
Just before the farm, take the gate on your
left and pass in front of the buildings,

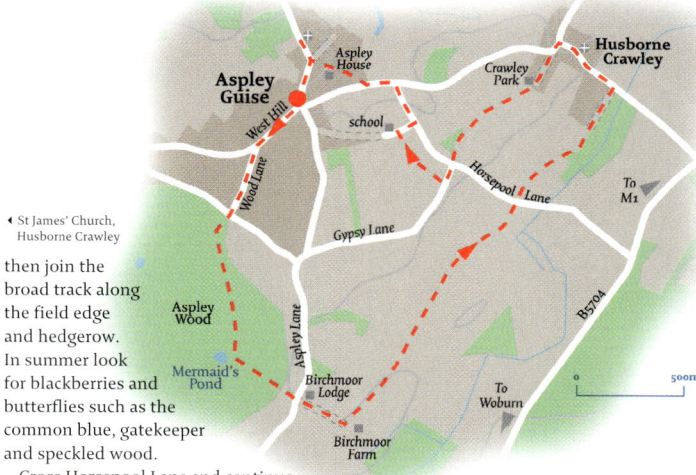

◀ St James' Church,
Husborne Crawley

then join the
broad track along
the field edge
and hedgerow.
In summer look
for blackberries and
butterflies such as the
common blue, gatekeeper
and speckled wood.

Cross Horsepool Lane and continue
straight on, emerging onto Crow Lane
beside a row of Bedford Estate cottages
known locally as the Duke of Bedford's
Mansions, built in 1853 to improve
accommodation for agricultural labourers.

On reaching the main road, turn left and
head uphill to reach Husborne Crawley
and St James' Church, beautifully sited
overlooking the surrounding valley and
partly built from locally quarried
greensand stone. Its eight bells are said to
be the finest sounding in the county.

Leaving the churchyard by the lychgate,
turn right, cross the road and take the
leftward curving path at the T-junction.
Continue through the Crawley Park
gateposts, along the gravel drive past The
Gardeners Cottage, through a gate and
onward beside parkland fencing, passing
some splendid mature trees.

Cross Horsepool Lane onto Gypsy Lane,
and beyond the houses take the
signposted footpath to the right. At the
village school, turn right, then left at the
next T-junction. Turn left at the main
road, cross over and after around 150m
follow Pickering Way to the right. To your
right look out for various sculptures, while
to the left catch glimpses of Aspley House
and its glorious gardens.

Once at the road, turn left to return to
The Square, but not before detouring right
to visit St Botolph's Church. Though the
site dates back to 1188, today's building is
of a largely Victorian flavour, with some
surviving 15th-century features.

With its conveniently located pub, The
Square is the perfect spot to reflect on
Dr Williams' assertion that the village has
a 'superior influence upon health'.

Woburn

Distance 11km **Time** 2 hours 30
Terrain pavements, field and woodland
paths, parkland **Map** OS Explorer 192
Access buses to Woburn from Leighton
Buzzard, Dunstable and Milton Keynes

**Well-to-do Woburn owes its existence to
the country house of Woburn Abbey that
has been the seat of the Dukes of Bedford
since 1547 and which is known today for
its superb surrounding parkland and
priceless collection of art and furniture.**

Turn left out of the car park in Park
Street, then turn right to wander
northwards up the High Street, admiring
the mix of historic buildings. At the bus
stop at Caswell Lane, take the bridleway
off to the left, at the end of which go left
and then right along the main road –
Leighton Street – for just under 500m.

Opposite Maryland on the right, go
through the gate signposted Greensand
Ridge Walk and carry on for around 750m:
up the track, straight on through a kissing
gate at the top of the rise and ahead across
the field, with a superb view of Woburn
Abbey opening up in front. The house was
originally a Cistercian monastery but was
disbanded by Henry VIII.

At the second intersection of paths go
left through a kissing gate and on through
the woods to the road. Continue to the
right and enter Woburn Abbey parkland
through a gate at Ivy Lodge. Follow the

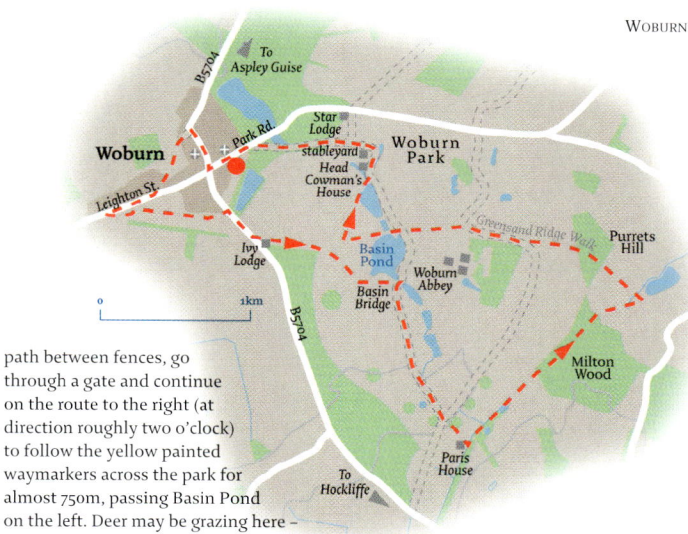

path between fences, go through a gate and continue on the route to the right (at direction roughly two o'clock) to follow the yellow painted waymarkers across the park for almost 750m, passing Basin Pond on the left. Deer may be grazing here – please don't approach the deer or try to feed them.

At the elegant arched stone bridge between the ponds, take a sharp right up the paved track and keep ahead for almost 1.25km. The path now runs through the trees to skirt Paris House round to the far side, then goes through a gate in the tall brick wall. In the field on the other side of the wall, go left and where a path joins from the right keep ahead for around 1.5km, signposted Woburn and Eversholt Circular Walk. In spring/early summer, look out for bright yellow brimstone butterflies, which lay their eggs on blackthorn.

At the end of this section, keep an eye open for the permissive path signs with waymarker arrows indicating the route to take across a field to an intersection of paths. Here, take the Greensand Ridge Walk for around 2.5km, heading left over a couple of bridges and then up and over Purrets Hill and back into Woburn Park. Red kites might be seen hereabouts.

Follow the waymarkers through the park, with Woburn Abbey on the left. Keep on down past the ponds, continuing ahead to an intersection of paths (almost back at the point where the route entered the park earlier), then take a sharp right to pass the quaint Head Cowman's House. Follow the path on around the stableyard, in front of the Bedford Office buildings and through the wooden gates on the other side of the grass. Continue ahead, passing a pond and some magnificent old sequoia trees to emerge on the main road into Woburn, at which turn left for the short stretch back to the start.

◀ Woburn's Old Town Hall

Milton Bryan and Eversholt

Distance 12km **Time** 3 hours
Terrain footpaths, fields and quiet lanes
Map OS Explorer 192 **Access** infrequent
buses to Milton Bryan from Leighton
Buzzard, Toddington and Milton Keynes

**Joseph Paxton, celebrated gardener,
architect and designer, was called
'England's busiest man' by Charles
Dickens. This walks takes in the gently
rolling Bedfordshire countryside and
grand estates where the great Victorian
began his career as a humble garden boy.**

From Milton Bryan's pretty South End,
take Pond Lane opposite the Red Lion
pub. For Bedfordshire, this is lofty ground
– its highest point stands around 160m
above sea level. At the second pond, take
the footpath across the field, bear right
and follow it to the road, where you cross
straight over to take the quiet lane for
around 1.2km to Battlesden. This tiny
hamlet is set amidst undulating
countryside – a patchwork of arable fields,
scattered farmsteads and pockets of
woodland. Look out for the distant white
lion carved into the chalk hillside of
Dunstable Downs. Passing Centre Farm,
the lane swings sharply right, running for
a further 800m to the hillside church of
St Peter and All Saints.

Take the footpath beside the gates of
Battlesden House, soon joining the broad
tree-lined expanse of Battlesden Avenue
for around 1.5km, once the formal
approach to a vast Gothic mansion.
Paxton would have walked here as a boy
on his way to work. He went on to become
head gardener of Chatsworth House,
designed Crystal Palace and, in later life,
landscaped the gardens at Battlesden.

Continue through the original estate
gates and turn left, following the road
verge with care for 250m. Turn right onto a
footpath running along the outer wall of
the Woburn Estate, ancestral home of the
Dukes of Bedford. After roughly 500m,
look out for Paris House, now a restaurant

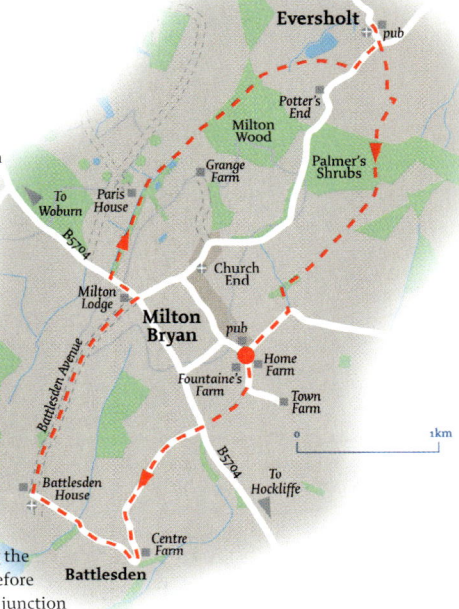

◀ Eversholt

but originally built for the 1878 Paris International Exhibition and transported here by the 9th Duke of Bedford.

Stay ahead on the footpath, which merges into a permissive woodland route, with a sharp left to rejoin the main footpath heading diagonally right. After crossing a wooden bridge into open grassland, follow the Greensand Ridge fingerpost through a plantation of oaks, known as a *quercetum*, home to 10 nationally important species from the genus *quercus* (oak).

At the road, turn left into Eversholt, a charming village made up of 13 'Ends', including the cheerfully named Witts End. Before taking the footpath at the road junction by the old School House, it's worth continuing ahead for the classic English village scene – cricket pitch, pub, church and pretty cottages – of Church End.

Taking the footpath near the old School House, cross the field and pass through a kissing gate. Skirting around two sides of the fenced-in field, continue across the grassland and through a second gate into the woods. Cross a wooden bridge and, at the fan of footpaths on the edge of the arable field, choose the third path heading diagonally right to the hedge corner and press on across the field.

Join a broad grass track that becomes a hedge-lined bridleway and follow it down to the road, at which turn right and return carefully to Milton Bryan. Beyond its rural calm, this tucked-away village played a secretive wartime role. During the Second World War, it hosted a covert 'black propaganda' radio station, operated by British agents posing as Germans. They broadcast fake news and the latest German hit tunes, aimed at undermining enemy morale – with intelligence gathered from nearby Bletchley Park helping to ensure the realism.

Marston Moretaine and Lidlington

Distance 10km **Time** 3 hours
Terrain footpaths, fields and hard-surface
paths **Maps** OS Explorer 192 and 208
Access buses to Marston Moretaine
from Bedford, Milton Keynes and
surrounding villages

It's hard to imagine this area was once a
feverishly busy industrial centre for brick
production, with its mass of chimneys
billowing smoke, enormous claypits and
huge workforce. Today's more peaceful
landscape of open fields, pretty villages
and the early shoots of a young forest
gives little sense of times past.

Start from Marston Moretaine's
St Mary's Church with its unusual
detached tower. Follow the path out the
back of the churchyard, over a small bridge
and then immediately right along the field
edge. After a short distance head
diagonally left by the waymarker post for

almost 2km over a few fields to the railway
line at Lidlington. For more than 100 years
the Marston Vale area was the centre of
Britain's brickmaking industry due to the
large belt of accessible Oxford clay
underfoot. If it's been raining or you're
walking in the middle of winter, be
warned – these fields will be very claggy.
There were once more than 160 towering
chimneys across the area and some 500
million bricks were produced annually at
the height of production. The post-war
building boom employed thousands and
workers from the south of Italy, Ukraine
and Poland, then later Pakistan and India,
came to help keep the furnaces firing.

At Lidlington cross the railway line and,
at the footpath, turn right for a loop of the
village. At the road go left, and right at the
T-junction by the village sign, then turn
right down Church Street (or ahead for the
pretty Green Man pub), before finally

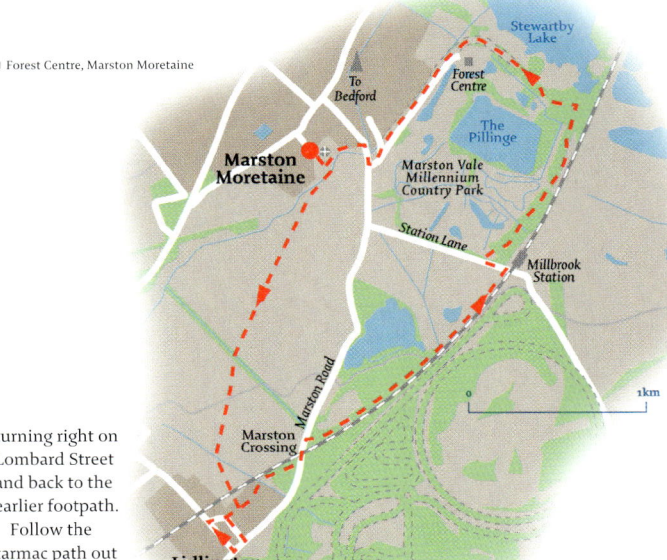

◄ Forest Centre, Marston Moretaine

turning right on Lombard Street and back to the earlier footpath.

Follow the tarmac path out of Lidlington and at Marston Road turn left, cross the railway and then almost immediately go right on the permissive footpath signposted as the Brick Route. Follow the path for around 1.5km as it winds through open grassy areas and trees, eventually arriving at Station Lane by Millbrook Station.

Cross the road and head on into the Millennium Country Park with its numerous trails, wetlands and woods. Take the hard-surface path to the right and follow the fingerposts for about 1.75km to the Forest Centre and café, visiting the viewpoint for a look at neighbouring Stewartby Lake along the way. This is the heart of the 158 sq km Forest of Marston Vale and is one of 12 community forests created in the UK during the early 1990s, with more than two million trees here. The wetlands trail around the lake known as The Pillinge is worth the admission fee, with its numerous hides, tower hide and woodland walkway (no dogs allowed).

From the forest centre head across the car park to rejoin the hard-surface path that runs parallel with the drive. Once at the country park entrance cross the road and head left to the T-junction, at which go right and then take the path on the left back to the church.

35

Ampthill

Distance 8km **Time** 2 hours
Terrain parkland, footpaths, fields and
pavement **Map** OS Explorer 193
Access buses to Ampthill from Bedford
and Milton Keynes

Once the favourite hunting seat of Henry
VIII, Ampthill today is a popular centre
enjoyed for its architecture and good mix
of independent shops and restaurants.
Despite its continued growth, it retains
the appealing air of a country village.

Starting from the edge of the town at the
Ampthill Great Park West car park, go
through the gate by the information board
and up the tree-lined Carriage Drive. Veer
right to Katherine's Cross, marking the
spot of the now long-gone 15th-century
castle where Henry VIII's first wife,
Katherine of Aragón, was confined during
their marriage annulment. The look and
feel of the park today is thanks largely to

the work of Lancelot 'Capability' Brown,
'England's greatest gardener', in the late
18th century.

Follow the clear gravel path eastwards
along the top with views north over
Marston Vale, where in the mid-20th
century the chimneys of the London
Brickworks Company stood 70m tall. The
last of the chimneys came down in 2021.
Off to the right is the Duke of Bedford
Cross, marking the site of the First World
War Ampthill Training Depot.

By the stand of spruce trees and timber
waymarker post leave the gravel path to
head diagonally left over the grass,
passing numerous benches, and continue
on through the gate into the woodland
(waymarked Heritage Trail). Follow the
path through the wood, at the T-junction
go right and at the road head left uphill.
Carefully cross the busy road to take the
concrete track for just over 1km to the

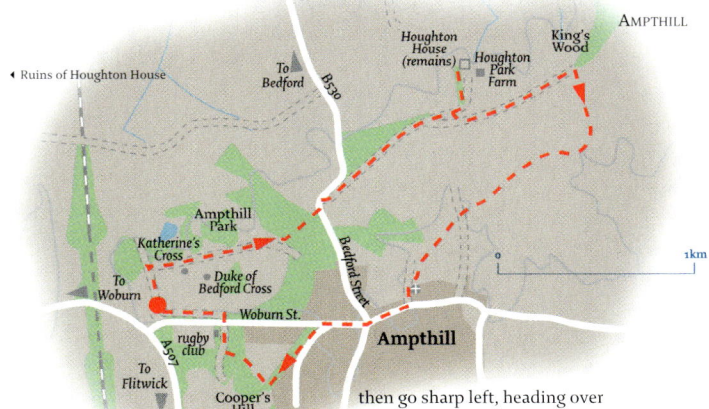

◀ Ruins of Houghton House

romantic ruins of Houghton House.

Commanding magnificent views over the surrounding countryside, this Jacobean- and Classical-style mansion, completed in 1621, was built for Mary, Countess of Pembroke and was reputedly the inspiration for John Bunyan's 'Palace Beautiful' in *The Pilgrim's Progress*.

Retracing your steps to the main track, turn right and then quickly left to follow the footpath behind the barns. Ignoring the 'Town Trail' path to the right, continue ahead over open countryside to a cottage and on to the southern tip of King's Wood, a Site of Special Scientific Interest due to its importance to wildlife. A wander around the woodland trails makes for a pleasant diversion.

At the corner of the wood, go through the kissing gate and take the footpath off to the right (signposted Greensand Ridge Walk), go through a kissing gate, following the hedge as it curves right and continue on through another gate and then go sharp left, heading over undulating countryside. Dropping down to the track, go left at the cattle grid and, if it's dry, take the path on the right across the field to the church. If it's wet continue down the track and turn right at the 'Town Trail' sign, then go through the cemetery leading to pretty St Andrew's Church and a square of almshouses.

Turning right at the road, wander into the heart of Georgian Ampthill. At the Town Pump cross over Bedford Street and head up Woburn Street, which runs behind the clocktower. After passing the Queen's Head pub, take the magnificent tree-lined walkway on the left, known as The Alameda, created by a landowner influenced by their travels in Spain.

At the end of the playing field and just before the war memorial follow the right-hand footpath skirting Cooper's Hill, Bedfordshire's largest remaining area of heathland and a mass of purple heather in late summer. Pass the rugby club and cross over Woburn Street to re-enter the Great Park, turning left for the car park.

Flitwick and Flitton Moors

Distance 8km **Time** 2 hours
Terrain pavement, footpaths and fields
Map OS Explorer 193 **Access** buses to
Flitwick from Bedford, Dunstable and
Milton Keynes; trains to Flitwick from
Bedford, Luton and London

**Escape the hustle and bustle of daily life
at Bedfordshire's largest natural wetland,
thriving with birds, dragonflies, lizards,
mosses and fungi. Along the way explore
the delightful village of Flitton, including
the extravagant mausoleum of the de
Greys of Wrest Park.**

Turn left out of Flitwick railway station,
then left again over the railway line and
diagonally right along Kings Road,
continuing ahead where it turns into
Greenfield Road. Take the footpath on the
left just after Flitwick Mill to leave behind
the noise of the traffic and instead enjoy
birdsong and the babbling River Flit.

At the path junction with the bench
continue ahead through the kissing gate,
following the river, and then on over the
open pasture to the green Wildlife Trust
noticeboard. Go through the kissing gate,
cross over the river, go through another
gate and then turn left along the bridleway
for a short distance before going right at
the waymarker post.

Crossing the field, continue on into
Flitton village, arriving at Brook Lane by
the picturesque Church of St John the
Baptist and White Hart pub. Before
turning left along Brook Lane, it's worth
exploring the church and, if open, the
mausoleum housing a remarkable
sequence of 17 sculpted and effigied
monuments, spanning nearly two and a
half centuries, to the de Grey family.

Pass the pretty cottages along Brook
Lane, which soon peters out and becomes
a footpath. Cross the river, then turn left

◀ Flit Valley Discovery Centre

in front of the Flit Valley Discovery Centre and immediately right to loop round three sides of Flitton Moor, a wetland created in the 1980s by the county council. Turn right to rejoin the main path which follows a straight canalised section of the River Flit. The river originally flowed in numerous channels through the large peat bog, but this section was redirected to a straight cutting in the 19th century.

Go left over the bridge and retrace your earlier steps along the bridleway, then turn right through the kissing gates at the start of the houses. This time, once over the River Flit, take the right-hand path diagonally over the grassy pasture. Go through the two consecutive metal gates and straight across the next field – the far end can be very boggy, so following the woodland edge to the right is sometimes required.

Turn right to enter the wet woodland and acidic grassland of Flitwick Moor. This is an important site for mosses with some 130 species and 500 recorded species of fungi. Cotton grass also grows here, which is more usually seen on upland peat bogs. The 'Flitwick Spring' water was once sold in Victorian and Edwardian London as an iron-rich blood tonic but the supply couldn't sustain the business and it finally folded in the 1930s – it would be a brave person to sup the waters today!

At the end of the wet woodland, turn left to take the track across the field, left onto Maulden Road and then right at the T-junction to return to Flitwick Station.

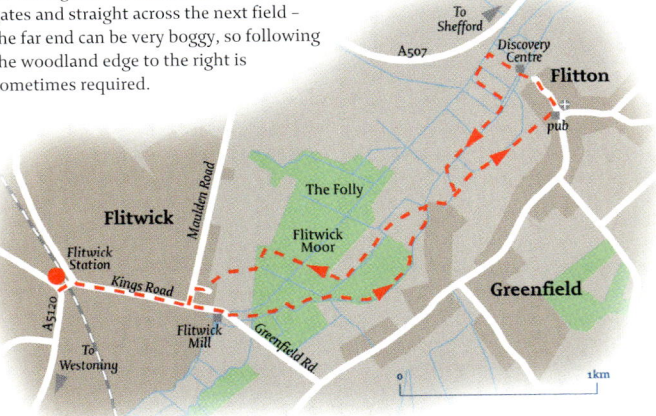

Sundon Hills and Sharpenhoe Clappers

Distance 9km **Time** 2 hours
Terrain footpaths, open grassland and lanes **Map** OS Explorer 193 **Access** no buses to Sundon Hills car park; can access the route via buses to Streatley and Upper Sundon from Luton

Whether you're a weathered hiker, wildlife enthusiast or seeking a mindful retreat, this classic ramble in the Chilterns National Landscape offers visitors an enchanting escape into nature.

From the Sundon Hills Country Park car park, stride along the grassy escarpment top, following the fenceline and hedge on the John Bunyan Trail. This is one of Bedfordshire's highest points, perfect for blowing away the cobwebs and offering stunning views toward Sharpenhoe Clappers and the countryside beyond. This chalk escarpment cutting across the county is steeped in nature, farming and

cultural heritage, and is home to rare bee and pyramidal orchids, a wide range of birds, and butterflies such as small heath and chalkhill blue.

At the end of the open grassland, turn right and follow the main path meandering along the top, keeping to the higher route where paths split. Go through a kissing gate, briefly descend, then climb steps into a magnificent beechwood. Keep to the right-hand path and, at the series of waymarker posts, leave the Bunyan Trail, keeping ahead on the Icknield Way Trail and following it between the wood and a field.

Pass through another kissing gate, cross the grassland and carefully cross the road into Sharpenhoe Clappers car park. Proceed ahead on the tarmac path, which soon becomes a grassy track. When the path splits, continue straight onto the Clappers, crowned by traces of an Iron Age

◄ Sundon Hills

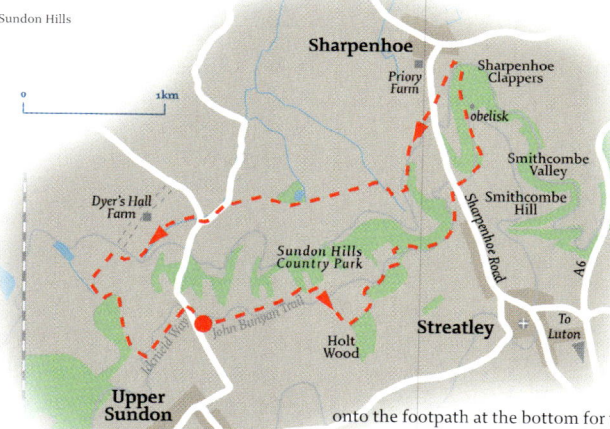

0   1km

Sharpenhoe

Priory
Farm

Sharpenhoe
Clappers

obelisk

Smithcombe
Valley

Smithcombe
Hill

Dyer's Hall
Farm

Sundon Hills
Country Park

Sharpenhoe Road

A6

 Icknield Way   John Bunyan Trail

Holt
Wood

Streatley

To
Luton

**Upper
Sundon**

hillfort and a striking beechwood shaped by prevailing winds. In the open grassy area, a well-placed bench offers a chance to soak in the view, watch red kites year-round or listen to summer skylarks and blackcaps. The origin of the name Clappers is unclear, but it is possibly derived from the Latin *claperius* or French *clapier*, meaning 'a heap of stones' or 'rabbit hole'. The site was adapted as a warren for rabbit farming in the 15th century to supply meat and skins.

Entering the woodland, trails fan out. Veer right for a fine beech avenue, straight ahead for the obelisk erected by William Alexander Robertson in memory of his two brothers killed in the First World War, or left along the woodland edge for valley glimpses. Each route meets at the far side to descend the steep steps, turning left

onto the footpath at the bottom for the return leg. Cross a field and a road to join a bridleway along the field edge flanked by a fine hedgerow on the left. Continue around to the right as the bridleway curves with the field boundary, then cross a bridge to follow the signposted Icknield Way straight ahead along the field edge, between a pond and small wood. Curve right up to a lane, at which you turn left. On reaching a T-junction, turn right, cross with care and take the signposted bridleway.

Following the waymarker posts past a smallholding, at the path T-junction turn left (no waymarker), then right at the metal 'access point' for a gentle climb up a tree-lined bridleway. Emerging onto open grassland, pass through a hedge on the left and follow the path to the road. Turn right briefly (the road has no pavement and can be busy), cross and take the Icknield Way path back to the car park.

Silsoe and Higham Gobion

Distance 9.5km **Time** 2 hours 30
Terrain footpath, fields and tracks
Map OS Explorer 193 **Access** buses to Silsoe
from Bedford and Luton

Silsoe owes much of its development to
neighbouring Wrest Park, for more than
600 years home to the aristocratic de Grey
family. The house is impressive while the
grounds and gardens, recently restored,
are magnificent.

From Silsoe's St James the Great Church,
head down Park Avenue, cross the A6
bypass bridge, and on entering Wrest Park
turn right to follow the broad hedge-lined
bridleway. Continue over Wrest Park's Old
Park, through Buckle Grove wood and
across the field to the road. If ploughed
and muddy, you can follow the track
around to the right.

Cross the road and continue on the
bridleway past Fielden Cottages, through
a small wood and along the field edge. In
autumn the hedgerow here is laden with
sloe berries. Go through the gap in the
bottom hedge, turn immediately left, then
after about 140m turn right, taking the
footpath (no waymarker) across the field
to the opposite hedge and over a small
footbridge. Cross another field, then go
left along the ditch and hedge, turning
right when it meets the grassy track.
Follow the track, soon becoming gravel,
then tarmac, through a veterinary complex
to the road.

This is the sleepy hamlet of Higham
Gobion, where historic earthworks have
been variously interpreted as the remains
of an early castle or the site of an old fish
farm. Perhaps more intriguingly, in the

◀ Wrest Park

17th century, the village vicar was Edmund Castell, a 17th-century Professor of Arabic at Cambridge and compiler of the *Lexicon Heptaglotton*, a dictionary of seven Middle Eastern languages. Despite working 18 hours a day over 18 years, employing 14 assistants and spending a small fortune, no-one bought his book when it was published, landing him in a debtors' prison.

Turn left to visit St Margaret's Church, of 12th-century origin but largely rebuilt in the Victorian era. Continue carefully along the road and, immediately after the last house, go left again onto the bridlepath and follow it for around 3km back to Wrest Park. This is initially along the field edge, then entering the site of the motte and bailey/fishponds, before continuing past fields and a small wood to the road. Cross straight over and follow the bridleway into Whitehall Plantation, looking up to spot the mistletoe-laden treetops. At the track T-junction, go left, exiting the wood at Whitehall Lodge, and continue ahead across the fields to the complex of buildings and workshops. Turn left at the

road and walk along the main drive of Wrest Park enjoying the grandeur of this château-style mansion house – a little bit of French flavour in the heart of Bedfordshire. Today cared for by English Heritage, it is well worth visiting for both the house and three centuries of English garden design, including a rare early 18th-century formal garden.

Once ready to depart, continue along the drive back to the start. The de Greys' impressive mausoleum can be visited at nearby Flitton.

Bedford

3 Blunham

1 Willington

Sandy

Potton

B1042

Stotfold Mill ▶

4 Sutton

5 Wrestlingworth

Northill

2

Biggleswade

Langford

7

Chicksands

8 Shefford

6 Stotfold

Meppershall

9

East Bedfordshire stretches out as an open landscape shaped by centuries of cultivation and quiet innovation. This is the county's agricultural heartland where, despite the rush of the modern age, market gardening and farming still define village life. These walks trace the gentle contours of the Ivel valley – an area of subtle charm.

Biggleswade, Sandy and Stotfold sit astride the historic Great North Road. Once an artery for stagecoaches and now subsumed in the busy A1, the noise of modern life is quickly left behind along tracks and paths that stretch out on either side. Here lies the largest expanse of commonland in the county, at

Biggleswade, while the nearby RSPB headquarters offers a wilder landscape.

The bucolic villages of Old Warden and Ickwell are among the prettiest in the area, with thatched cottages and ancient greens – Ickwell's maypole is still the scene of May Day dancing. In Moggerhanger, meanwhile, stands a rare example of a Sir John Soane-designed house. The area has also produced notable figures: Thomas Tompion, the celebrated clockmaker, hailed from Ickwell, while Dan Albone, of Biggleswade, revolutionised farming with his pioneering tractor designs.

From historic packhorse bridges to sand hills and Roman roads, East Bedfordshire is brimming with intriguing diversions.

East Bedfordshire

1 **Cople and Willington** 46
A gentle stroll through fields and
historic village corners, complete
with a church and a dovecote

2 **Northill, Ickwell and Old Warden** 48
From maypoles to flying machines,
thatched cottages to regal carvings,
this walk is full of unusual treats

3 **Blunham, Great Barford
and Tempsford** 50
A walk of three riverside villages,
each with its own historical tales of
trade, faith and flight

4 **Potton, Biggleswade
and Sandy Heath** 52
Explore these eastern reaches,
where birdlife flourishes, commons
stretch wide and bridges whisper of
packhorse days

5 **Cockayne Hatley
and Wrestlingworth** 54
Surprising connections with a
children's classic on this easy route

6 **Stotfold Mill and the River Ivel** 56
A short walk with watery charm,
working heritage and wildlife aplenty

7 **Henlow and Langford** 58
Keep an eye open for otters in a
riverside nature reserve

8 **Shefford and Campton** 60
Explore countryside where
monasteries gave way to air bases
and a poet found his voice

9 **Meppershall and Shillington** 62
A walk of valley views, water
meadows and one of Bedfordshire's
finest churches

Cople and Willington

Distance 14km **Time** 3 hours 30
Terrain pavement, footpaths, cyclepath
and quiet lanes **Map** OS Explorer 208
Access buses to Cople from Bedford
and Biggleswade

From Danish occupation to Hollywood blockbusters, big skies to watery habitats, this less well-known route offers up a few surprises – not to mention a village pub and riverside café.

From the parking area at Cople's 15th-century All Saints Church head southeast along Northill Road, past the Five Bells pub and Woodlands Close, and out to the edge of the village. Turn right and keep on down Water End for almost 1.5km, passing thatched and Bedford Estate cottages, a reminder that the Dukes of Bedford were Lords of the Manor of Cople until 1902. At the gate across the lane continue ahead to a farm, at which go through the gate on the right and then immediately left to follow the fenceline.

Go through the gate between the farmhouse and pond, on through another gate and along the centre of the broad wildflower meadow, lined with blackthorn and hawthorn. Birdsong is all that can be heard – no matter the time of year, listen out for yellowhammer (with their 'little bit of bread and no cheese' call). Go through the gate at the end of the meadow into a small wood and, at the path T-junction, turn left and continue straight ahead along the edge of four fields.

On reaching the road turn left, keeping to the broad verge for about 600m and taking in views to the west, over to the left, of the giant hangars at Cardington. Originally built for the construction of airships such as the ill-fated *R101*, today they are used as film studios, ideal for building massive sets. *Star Wars, Batman*

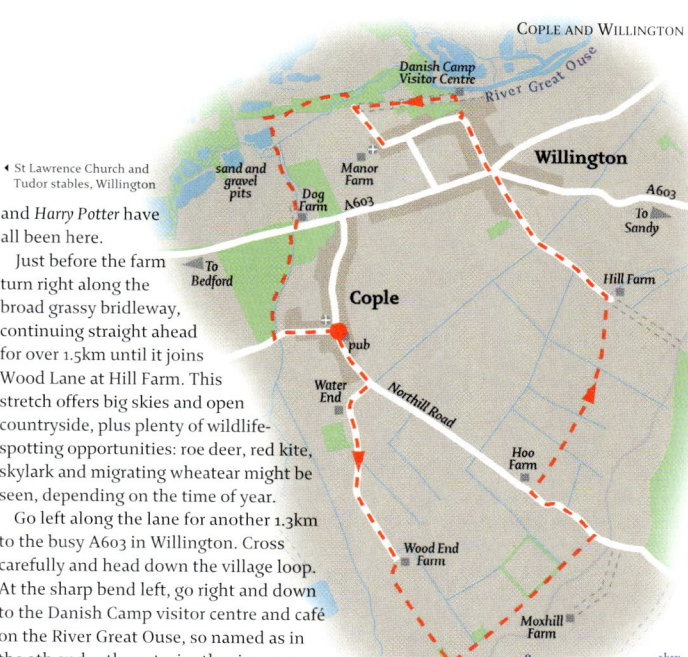

◀ St Lawrence Church and
Tudor stables, Willington

and *Harry Potter* have
all been here.

Just before the farm
turn right along the
broad grassy bridleway,
continuing straight ahead
for over 1.5km until it joins
Wood Lane at Hill Farm. This
stretch offers big skies and open
countryside, plus plenty of wildlife-
spotting opportunities: roe deer, red kite,
skylark and migrating wheatear might be
seen, depending on the time of year.

Go left along the lane for another 1.3km
to the busy A603 in Willington. Cross
carefully and head down the village loop.
At the sharp bend left, go right and down
to the Danish Camp visitor centre and café
on the River Great Ouse, so named as in
the 9th and 10th centuries the river was a
vital highway for Viking armies, allowing
them to penetrate deep into England.

Leave the Danish Camp and turn right
along the cyclepath, following the route of
the old Oxford to Cambridge Varsity Line,
which closed in 1968 (the station platform
can still be seen). At the timber fingerpost
the walk route goes right, but it's worth a
mini detour left up to the Tudor dovecote
and stables, in the care of the National
Trust, and the Church of St Lawerence,
regarded as one of the county's finest
Perpendicular churches.

Retrace your steps to the cyclepath, cross

Elstow Brook and go left at the fingerpost
along the earth track through the wood.
Go left at the next fingerpost (signed for
the A603/Cople) along a grassy track,
passing old gravel pits now returned to
nature as a watery habitat. Cross the brook
and continue along to Dog House and the
busy A603 road. Carefully cross over onto
the bridleway directly opposite and stay
with the path through the scrubby
woodland and pools which are great for
wildlife. Once at the lane turn left and
follow this back to the start.

Northill, Ickwell and Old Warden

Distance 13km **Time** 3 hours
Terrain footpaths, fields and pavement
Map OS Explorer 208 **Access** bus to Northill
from Bedford, Biggleswade and Hitchin

Aviation enthusiasts – and fans of *Those
Magnificent Men in their Flying Machines* –
are in for a treat on this loop around
three bucolic villages that also skirts
Shuttleworth Airfield. Not only was the
classic 1965 film partly made in the area,
but Shuttleworth is home to a superb
collection of airworthy vintage aircraft.

Start from St Mary's Church in pretty
Northill, with its attractive cottages, pub
and 14th-century church set around a
picturesque pond. The clock on the church
tower is by Thomas Tompion, the 'Father
of English Clockmaking', who was born in
neighbouring Ickwell in 1639.

Walk past the pond along Ickwell Road
for around 800m to Ickwell and one of the
few surviving large greens in the county,
complete with red and white striped
maypole. Follow the left-hand edge of the
green, cross Caldecote Road – the white
thatched cottage over to the left is
Tompion's birthplace – and leave the
village via The Sheepwalk bridleway.

At Hill Lane cross straight over and
follow the bridleway winding around the
edge of the airfield, part of Shuttleworth
Estate. Created in 1802 by Lord Ongley and
purchased in 1872 by Joseph Shuttleworth,
the estate was inherited by Richard
Ormonde Shuttleworth, who was killed
in an aviation accident in 1940 at the age
of 31. His mother Dorothy founded a
charitable trust in his memory, which
includes Shuttleworth House, Swiss
Garden and a world-renowned collection
of aeroplanes and vintage cars.

Continue along the bridleway, turning
right onto the main estate road, then left
after 100m to follow the waymarked
bridleway – look out for the old ploughs.

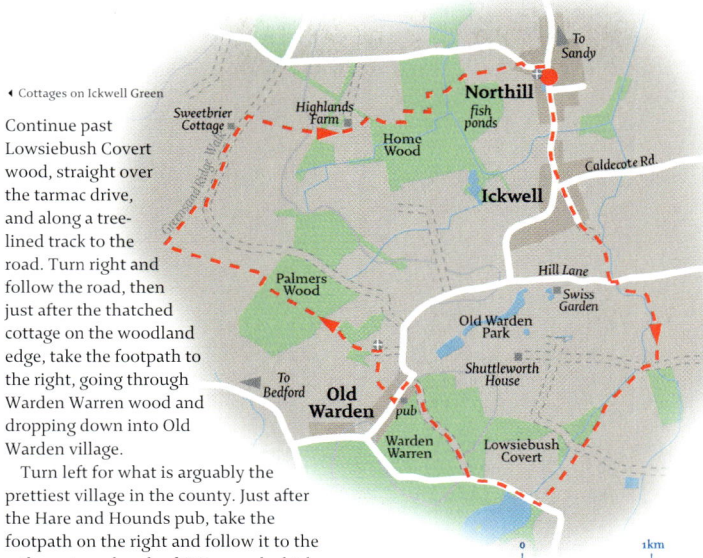

◀ Cottages on Ickwell Green

Continue past Lowsiebush Covert wood, straight over the tarmac drive, and along a tree-lined track to the road. Turn right and follow the road, then just after the thatched cottage on the woodland edge, take the footpath to the right, going through Warden Warren wood and dropping down into Old Warden village.

Turn left for what is arguably the prettiest village in the county. Just after the Hare and Hounds pub, take the footpath on the right and follow it to the 12th-century church of St Leonard which contains fine carved woodwork, including some believed to originate from the chapel of Anne of Cleves in Bruges (there are entwined AC carvings on the altar).

Turn left and leaving the top of the car park via the footpath, continue on for around 1km through the centre of Palmers Wood. At the far edge of the wood, turn right, then left, following the field boundary over a small timber bridge and up to join the Greensand Ridge Walk. The final stage of this walk follows the Greensand Ridge Walk for almost 4km back to Northill. Turn right along the bridleway leading around the field edge (it can be muddy), looking left over the valley to Bedford and the massive Cardington Hangars. Cross over a stone bridge, then go left along a broad tree-lined track.

Just after the house in the woods (Sweetbrier Cottage), turn right along a field-edge path, go on through a tree belt and cross a paddock around the distinctive Georgian farmhouse of Highlands Farm. Continue through the small wood, along a field edge path, and follow the Greensand Ridge Walk signs through Home Wood. Leaving the wood via a kissing gate, the route passes some medieval fishponds. Follow the path between the paddocks to Bedford Road, where you turn right to return to the start.

Blunham, Great Barford and Tempsford

Distance 11.5km **Time** 3 hours
Terrain footpaths and pavements
Map OS Explorer 208 **Access** infrequent
buses to Blunham from Bedford,
Biggleswade and St Neots

**This walk encompasses three riverside
villages, each with a fine church, and a
classic Bedfordshire view. Be aware that
the route can flood at numerous spots
after very wet weather, in summer there
are lots of stinging nettles and you are
likely to encounter cattle.**

From the bottom of The Hill in
Blunham follow the High Street past
characterful cottages, The Horseshoes pub
with stately St Edmund or St James
Church tucked behind it, and John Donne
Primary School. One of the finest
metaphysical poets of the 17th century,
Donne was Rector of Blunham from 1621
to 1631 while simultaneously serving as
Dean of St Paul's Cathedral in London.

When the High Street bends to the right
take the waymarked footpath on the left
(Gt Barford Lock), keeping ahead on the
hedge-lined track. Go under the pylon, left
at the waymarker, crossing a stream, and
continue along a track, following the
waymarker posts left, then right to one of
Bedfordshire's classic views: the 15th-
century 17-arched bridge at Great Barford
crossing the Great Ouse, punctuated by
moored boats, The Anchor pub and the
tower of All Saints Church.

Cross the footbridge over the lock, go
left and at the pub turn right to follow the
road verge with care for roughly 500m to
take the bridleway on the right around
and down to the river. This is part of the
Ouse Valley Way and is also a good area
for wildlife. Come at dawn or dusk and
you might catch a glimpse of an otter, but
also look – and listen – out for ducks,
overwintering geese, the sweet song of
returning warblers in spring, and beautiful

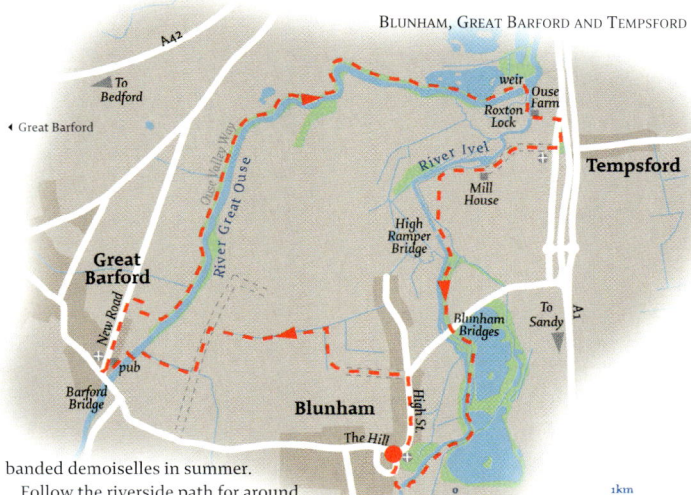

To
Bedford

◄ Great Barford

weir
Ouse
Farm
Roxton
Lock

River Ivel

Tempsford

Ouse Valley Way

River Great Ouse

Mill
House

High
Ramper
Bridge

Great
Barford

New Road

Blunham
Bridges

To
Sandy

pub

Barford
Bridge

Blunham

High St.

The Hill

0   1km

banded demoiselles in summer.

Follow the riverside path for around 3.5km to Roxton Lock, at which cross the river, go through the kissing gate and continue onto the Kingfisher Way on the River Ivel. After a short distance take the bridge to the left over the river, following the waymarkers through the yard of Ouse Farm (being mindful of the resident cattle) and along to the Tempsford village road. Enter the Tempsford Millennium Garden Sanctuary through the mighty lion-topped pillars and heavy gate on the left. The garden was created at the old entrance to Tempsford Hall on land compulsory purchased in the 1960s for the development of the A1 trunk road. Follow the trail through the garden, exiting at the war memorial, and cross over the road onto Mill Lane, with options to visit the Wheatsheaf pub and/or St Peter's Church, both situated at this junction. The latter houses memorials to agents who took on espionage, sabotage and reconnaissance missions in Nazi-occupied Europe during the Second World War, and who were flown out from nearby RAF Tempsford at night by the RAF's 'moon' squadrons.

The tarmac of Mill Lane soon gives way to gravel. Pass to the right of Mill House, go through a kissing gate and left along the field edge. Cross the footbridge over a stream and, at the River Ivel, don't cross but keep following the left bank.

Cross the road with double bridges to continue ahead on the riverside footpath for 1.3km, soon picking up glimpses of Blunham and the church tower. Cross at the weir, with a fine view of the church and old rectory, and continue through an area known as The Trap (once a site of commercial eel trapping) and along Park Lane back to the start.

Potton, Biggleswade and Sandy Heath

Distance 15km **Time** 3 hours 30
Terrain footpaths, fields and pavements
Map OS Explorer 208 **Access** bus to Potton
from Bedford, Sandy and Biggleswade

In the 11th century, Potton formed
part of the Hundred of Weneslawe, which
lends its name to the Weneslawe Walk
that tours the historic district and is
followed for most of this route.

From Brook End in Potton, turn left out
of the car park, left at the T-junction, then
right just after the fire station (signposted
Sutton) along Potton Brook. Take a sharp
left after the final house and follow the
fenceline, which shortly heads into the
woodland. At the waymarker post, follow
the North Beds Heritage Trail through the
wood, then continue along a broad riding
that edges Pegnut Wood, planted in the
mid-1990s with poplar trees that look
particularly colourful in autumn. Continue
along a field edge, then on ahead over a
field to join the High Street in Sutton. Turn

right and shortly reach the John O'Gaunt
pub. The route continues down a
bridleway to the left, signposted
Greensand County, but it's worth a short
detour ahead to see Bedfordshire's only
packhorse bridge, dating from the late
13th or early 14th century. Cross the bridge
for a fine view of the Old Rectory and
All Saints Church.

Back at the bridleway, known locally as
Lantern Lane, follow this long straight
path across farmland for approximately
1.5km to a small wood, where it joins a
farm track. In summer, listen for skylarks
overhead and in winter charms of finches
in the branches. Stay with the track as it
curves sharply right but continue straight
ahead on the grassy field edge to the trees
when it goes sharply left.

Cross the bridge into Biggleswade
Common, continuing ahead through the
trees before following the hedge/fenceline
around to exit at the roundabout. Turn
right along Baden Powell Way and then

◀ Bridleway through
RSPB reserve, Sandy

left at the roundabout with the King's Reach pub along Potton Road for 500m, before taking the bridleway on the right marked with a fingerpost. Keep ahead for just over 1.25km, initially passing between houses and then crossing over farmland. You then re-enter and cross Biggleswade Common, the largest area of commonland in Bedfordshire, where local farmers have the right to graze cattle and horses.

In around 500m, after crossing the stream, the path goes over the former Sandy and Potton Railway branchline and enters the RSPB Lodge Reserve, headquarters of one of the country's largest charities. Unless you're a member, stay with the bridleway, passing through a lovely woodland of oak, Scots pine and silver birch, full of birds such as nuthatches, woodpeckers and jays. Continue along the main driveway up to the Swiss-style gatehouse (RSPB shop, toilets and café) at the road.

Cross the main road and carry on up a bridleway, then turn right by the pylon onto Long Riding, an oak-fringed track that runs perfectly straight for approximately 1.5 km. At the end, go right

at the T-junction, through the wood and along the driveway, passing the Sandy Heath transmitter. Where the drive bends sharply right at Dirok house, continue ahead on the waymarked path, soon becoming a hard-surface path back to Potton. At the road, turn right down Newtown, then left along Sandy Road at the mini roundabout. Continue ahead for around 750m, following the road around to the left to the pretty market square, full of independent shops. Exit via Brook End in the right-hand corner of the square to return to the car park.

53

Cockayne Hatley and Wrestlingworth

Distance 9km **Time** 2 hours
Terrain country lanes, rough tracks and
field paths **Map** OS Explorer 208
Access buses to Cockayne Hatley from
Sandy and Biggleswade

The Victorian poet and critic W E Henley
was a regular visitor to Cockayne Hatley.
A friend of J M Barrie, his daughter
Margaret was the inspiration for Wendy
in *Peter Pan*, while his poem *Invictus* has
become synonymous with Nelson
Mandela, who quoted it to other prisoners
on Robben Island. A large memorial in the
middle of the churchyard at the start of
this walk marks the final resting place of
both Henley and Margaret.

Start from St John the Baptist Church,
just west of the village, where there is
space for one or two cars in the verge.
With your back to the church, go left and
then left again through a kissing gate
between two fields. Emerging shortly after
on the quiet main road, continue left all
the way through the village and out the
other side, keeping ahead on an obvious
track signposted Clopton Way where the
road runs out.

Stay on the track for around 1km, round
a bend to the right, then left. Keep ahead
and continue on a permissive footpath
across the top of a field, on the other side
of which turn right where the path splits,
keeping the hedge and ditch on your left.
In winter this stretch is a mass of rosehips,
providing shelter and food for hungry
birds. It also marks the boundary with
neighbouring Cambridgeshire.

Follow the line of the hedge for around
1km before turning left, then right. Cross
bridges over two ditches in quick
succession, followed shortly after by a

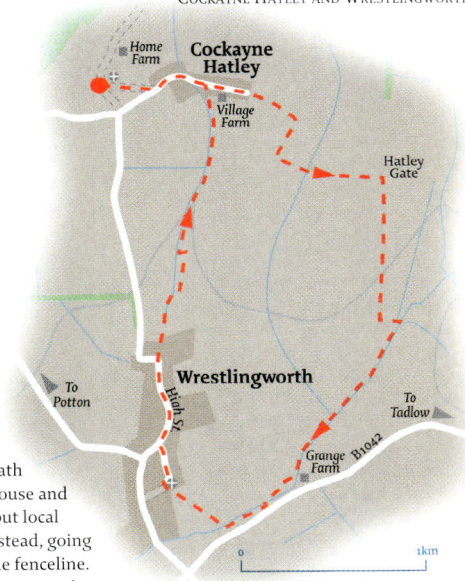

◀ St John the Baptist
Church, Cockayne Hatley

third, and ignore paths
going off left and right.
On reaching a fenceline
bearing right, the official path
continues ahead round a house and
through a private garden, but local
walkers skirt the garden instead, going
right and then left along the fenceline.

Just past the private driveway on the
other side of the house, make for a large
wooden garage/shed building
immediately ahead, behind which, hidden
from view, is the first of several kissing
gates. The route winds its way across a
field, over a ditch and right along a couple
more fields. Then go right again to re-cross
the ditch and head diagonally up the field
to another kissing gate in the top left
corner, emerging on a quiet lane by the
delightful 14th-century church of St Peter
in Wrestlingworth in a peaceful setting,
tucked away in a corner surrounded by
cottages. Wrestlingworth has a gruesome
claim to fame as the home in the 19th
century of 'The Potton Poisoner', one

Sarah Dazley, who was convicted and
hanged at Bedford Gaol for the murder of
her husband.

From the church, follow the road down
to the High Street, then go right for
around 500m. Where the High Street
bends sharply to the left and becomes
Hatley Road, keep ahead on a signposted
public footpath up the side of a house for
around 1.5km. Turn right, then left at an
intersection of paths after which keep the
ditch on your left. Soon the tower of
St John the Baptist Church at Cockayne
Hatley comes into view. Keep ahead into
the village, turning left along the lane to
retrace your steps to the start.

Stotfold Mill and the River Ivel

Distance 4km **Time** 1 hour
Terrain footpaths and quiet lanes
Map OS Explorer 193 **Access** buses to
Stotfold from Shefford, Hitchin
and Letchworth

Stotfold lies close to the boundary
between Bedfordshire and Hertfordshire,
a location which has been known to cause
confusion over the years, not least
because its postal town is Hitchin, in
Hertfordshire. Nonetheless, this gentle
amble around the meadows of the upper
reaches of the River Ivel is definitely on
the Bedfordshire side of the border.

The Ivel rises just over the county
boundary in Baldock and flows for about
25km through Bedfordshire, joining the
River Great Ouse at Roxton Lock near
Tempsford. The area is rich in flora and
fauna, and this route also includes some
of Stotfold's oldest buildings. The name
Stotfold is derived from 'stock fold', as
this was a popular stopping point for
livestock being driven from the north to
the London markets.

From the car park at Malthouse Lane,
turn left and away from Stotfold, go over
the small bridge and on past Centenary
Wood on the right. At the road junction go
right onto Mill Lane, which is lined with
hedgerow trees of hawthorn, blackthorn
and elder alive with insects and birds.

Continue down the lane for just over
500m, passing the cemetery with its small
Victorian chapel and, as the road curves
right, enter the Stotfold Mill Local Nature

Reserve on the left. This eight-acre site of wild meadow, native trees and numerous ponds can be fully explored via the 1.5km circular path. Early spring brings the distinctive snake's-head fritillary, while in the warmer months of June and July look out for bee orchids, Bedfordshire's county flower. Mute swan, heron, kingfisher and, if you're lucky, elusive otter might be spotted all year round.

Back at the road turn left and, if you visit during one of the seasonal open days, you can pop in and explore the mill, shop and tearoom. The mill has an inspiring story of community spirit, not just in its social history and industrial fabric, but also in the more recent foundation of the Stotfold Mill Preservation Trust after a disastrous fire in the 1990s. Restored by the Trust's volunteers, the 4.2m-wide overshot cornmill waterwheel is the widest in the country. At the time of the Domesday Book in 1086 Stotfold had four mills with a combined rent, payable to Hugh de Beauchamp, Baron of Bedford, of £4 and 400 eels – a quantity that would be unlikely today now that they are critically endangered.

Continue along Mill Lane to reach the T-junction and turn right along Rook Tree Lane. After about 75m take the footpath on the left by the postbox for a detour to the beautifully situated St Mary's Church. Its oldest parts date to the 12th century, but like many English medieval churches it is an accumulation of additions spanning the centuries.

Retrace your steps back to Rook Tree Lane and cross directly over to take another footpath that leads through to and across Millennium Green. Continue ahead and at the corner with the school go diagonally right, crossing the meadow, heading for the yellow marker. Follow the path northwards along the banks of the River Ivel back to Malthouse Lane, at which go left to return to the start.

Henlow and Langford

Distance 11km **Time** 2 hours 30
Terrain pavement, field paths and tracks
Maps OS Explorer 193 and 208 **Access** bus
to Henlow from Bedford, Stevenage,
Hitchin, Cambridge, Biggleswade, Welwyn
Garden City and St Albans

Connected by the River Ivel as it wends
northwards to join the Great Ouse at
Tempsford, the neighbouring villages of
Henlow and Langford bookend this easy-
to-follow well-waymarked ramble.

From the parking area at the Millennium
Meadows Community Nature Reserve car
park down Gardeners Lane, head off
through the churchyard of St Mary's and
then go left down the road, passing
through the gates of the Church of
England secondary school and along the
path down the left of the metal fencing.
Take the first path on the left to cross the
river and then go left along the track,
skirting Poppy Hill Fishing Lakes, for just
over 750m.

Shortly after crossing a bridge over a
ditch, take the waymarked path going
gently uphill on the right, and make your
way over the railway bridge by going left
along the paved track at the top of the
path and then right up a path between
fences. On the other side of the railway, as
you descend the steps from the bridge, the
route continues half-left ahead into a field
and then right for around 250m before
cutting across the field on the left to a
waymarker by a small brick building.

Continue straight on across another two
fields along the southern edge of Langford
Solar Farm. At the end of the third field go
right and then left across a fourth field,

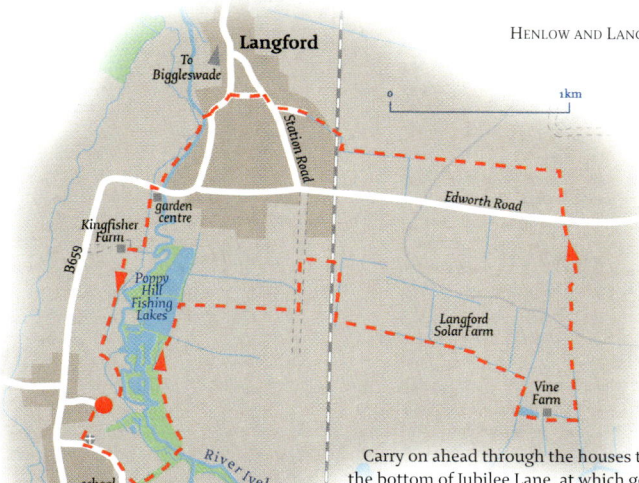

following the edge as it rounds to the right at the end before crossing a bridge over the ditch on your left. Keep to the path as waymarked around a private fishing pond and then continue ahead along a track past the farm buildings on your left. At a waymarked junction of tracks, go left, gently uphill, for over 1km.

As the path rises, fine views open up to the southwest of the Sharpenhoe Clappers chalk escarpment and Barton Hills. At the Edworth road, cross over carefully and continue straight across the field. Turn left down the path between trees for just over 1.25km to the pedestrian crossing over the main East Coast railway line. Follow the signposted instructions here and, taking great care, cross over when it is safe to do so.

Carry on ahead through the houses to the bottom of Jubilee Lane, at which go right and, soon after, left along The Leys. Continue left down the High Street for 150m and then cross a bridge over the river on the right, where otters are sometimes seen. Turn immediately left to follow the course of the river and at the main road cross over, go right and then, just past the garden centre, take the waymarked route on the left, signposted for Millennium Fields. Egret might be spotted in the fields here, making the most of the proximity of the Poppy Hill Fishing Lakes passed earlier, which are now just over to your left.

Follow the path down the field. At Kingfisher Farm turn left down the next field. Where the path splits, take the route through the gap in the hedge and bear left to cross the ditch. Continue following the line of the ditch to the right and waymarkers through Henlow Millennium Meadows Community Nature Reserve back to the start.

Shefford and Campton

Distance 7km **Time** 2 hours
Terrain pavement and footpaths
Map OS Explorer 193 **Access** buses to
Shefford from Bedford, Flitwick,
Biggleswade and Hitchin

The Rivers Flit and Hit link the market
town of Shefford to the pretty village of
Campton and Chicksands immediately
to the west. MOD Chicksands is home
to the Intelligence Corps, a small part of
the British Army which has a big impact
on decision making.

From the car park on Old Station Way in
Shefford, cut down to the High Street via
Duck Lane at the northeast end, go left
and then left again to follow Northbridge
Street to the River Flit. Along the way
admire The Porch, a 15th-century brick and
oak-beamed arcaded building, and look
out on the left at nos 17-19 for a plaque to
the pastoral poet Robert Bloomfield, who
spent his final years here. He is
remembered in particular for his poem,
The Farmer's Boy (1800), which celebrated
both the beauty and hardships of rural life
with its realistic, detailed portrayal of
agricultural work and the natural world.

After crossing the Flit, take the riverside
path to the left, its bank lined with
weeping willows, and follow it up
Riverside (a street) to Bedford Road. Turn
left, head out of Shefford and then take
the footpath on the left. Go under the old
railway bridge and follow the waymarkers
around the farmyard and up to the A600.
Carefully cross this busy road and
continue on the right-hand permissive
path, going straight ahead. This soon runs
alongside a narrow wood to the perimeter
fence of MOD Chicksands. In times past

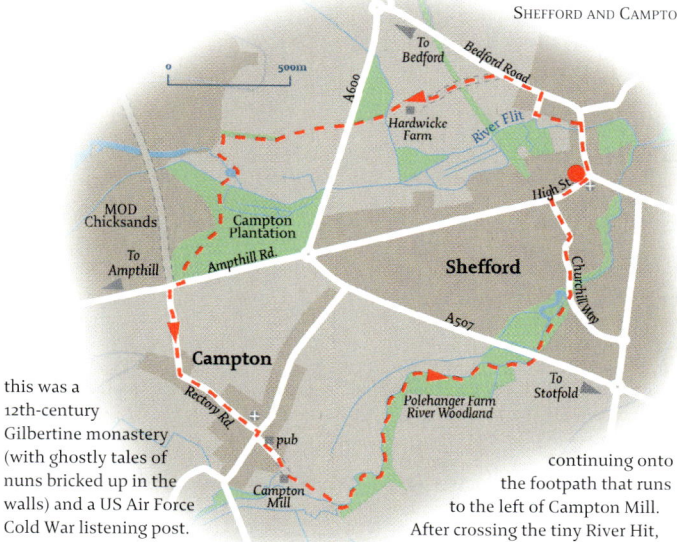

this was a 12th-century Gilbertine monastery (with ghostly tales of nuns bricked up in the walls) and a US Air Force Cold War listening post.

Taking the left-hand bridleway, follow the field edge, cross two bridges and carry on through Campton Plantation wood. The first part is known as Lower Alders, an increasingly scarce habitat of coppiced wet woodland, rich in insects, birds and bats. At the waymarker follow the right-hand bridleway to the A507 road, passing various chainsaw-carved sculptures and totem pole along the way.

Cross at the pedestrian crossing and head left down the road leading to Campton village, initially on Priory Road and then left along Rectory Road. Pass pretty cottages and All Saints Church, where poet Robert Bloomfield is buried. At the road junction go straight ahead onto Mill Lane, past the charming White Hart pub and down the lane, before continuing onto the footpath that runs to the left of Campton Mill.

After crossing the tiny River Hit, pass Curly's Seat and follow the riverside footpath along the edge of Polehanger Farm River Woodland, planted in 2000 with some 14,000 native trees to create a sustainable community outdoor space.

Continue under the A507 and straight ahead through Walkers Green. Turn left at the road (Churchill Way) and follow it for around 500m through the housing estate back to Shefford High Street. Turning right, wander back along the High Street to the start, passing a number of historic buildings: prominent St Francis Court, a group of Victorian buildings attached to the St Francis Roman Catholic Church; the 17th-century Tudor House at nos 36–38; and St Michael and All Angels Church, where part of the tower dates back to the 14th century.

Meppershall and Shillington

Distance 9.5km **Time** 2 hours 30
Terrain footpaths, fields and pavements
Map OS Explorer 193 **Access** infrequent
buses to Meppershall from Luton,
Shefford and Hitchin

Explore the charms of three villages
on this delightful walk through
quintessential English countryside past
historic churches, across farmland lined
with hedgerows and with sweeping valley
views. Nature is all around: red kites
overhead, the 'laughing' call of green
woodpecker and the summer song of
skylarks and yellowhammers.

Start from 12th-century St Mary's Church
in Meppershall, which for its size is
unusual in being of cruciform shape. From
the churchyard there is a good view of the
neighbouring magnificent half-timbered
17th-century manor. Take the footpath
opposite the churchyard entrance and

keep heading around to the left, through
the kissing gate, to follow the path along
the field edge. Where the path heads left
and right, take the right-hand path that
continues straight ahead along the field
edge, dropping down the hill.

Nip over the small bridge, then go
immediately right to continue along the
side of the ditch and the left-hand side of
the wood. Carry on through the kissing
gate and head diagonally left over the
water meadow, aiming for the metal gate
and Cow Bridge which, as the name
suggests, gave access to the grazing
meadows over the River Hit. Continue
ahead through a kissing gate and then
walk to the right, up the incline, into
Upper Gravenhurst.

At the road, turn left and just after the
12th-century St Giles Church take the
footpath on the left between houses. Head
down for around 500m, first past the

◄ All Saints Church, Shillington

houses and gardens, then along a track crossing open fields. Fine views abound with Lower Gravenhurst Church off to the right and ahead, in the distance, Shillington's All Saints Church, described by Sir John Betjeman as the 'Cathedral of the Chilterns'.

At the hedgerow, cross the ditch, take a quick left and then right to continue following the field edge. In the corner, ignore the footpath going off right to Lower Gravenhurst and instead continue around the field to follow the footpath, crossing the footbridge over the River Hit, then southeast on past the sewage works and adjacent earthwork remains thought to be a medieval moated site.

Pass along the side of the houses, through a metal kissing gate, straight over the driveway at the road and through the wooden kissing gate opposite to follow the grassy footpath to the right, which soon becomes a rubble track. Go left at the waymarker post to follow the footpath between a ditch and fenceline and over a bridge before continuing to the left along the edge of a field. Crossing the road, take the path ahead over two fields, across a bridge, through the kissing gate and along the right-hand edge of the meadow.

Turn left along the broad bridleway that climbs up to the Church of All Saints

Shillington, from where there are commanding views over the vale and a perfectly placed bench for a pitstop. Follow the path through the churchyard, along the back of the houses and down to the road. Turn left and follow Bury Road through Shillington for just over 1km, then take the footpath ahead for Shillington Bury at the T-junction. The path passes in front of the Bury, historically the principal seat of the Manor of Shillington, crosses a wooden bridge and then goes right to follow first the hedgerow, then a track across a field towards the trees. At the hedge, turn left and then right to rejoin the outbound path back to the start.

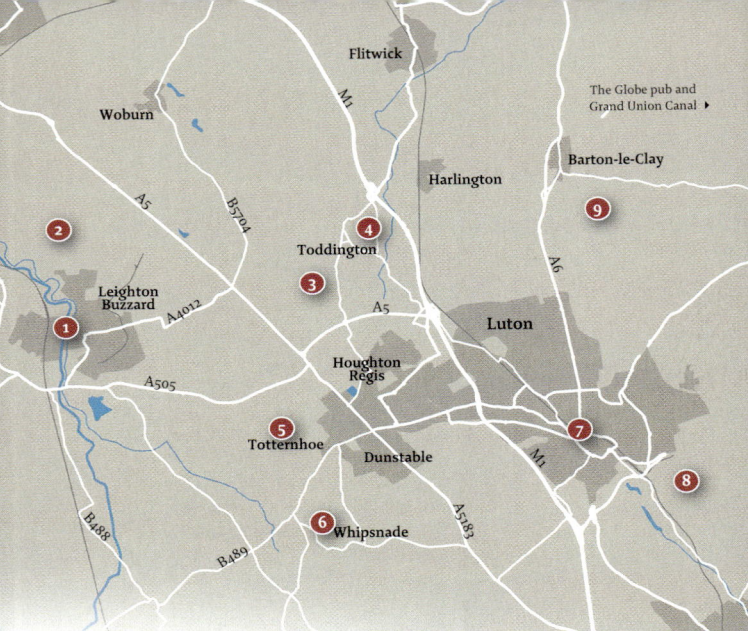

The Globe pub and
Grand Union Canal ▶

Flitwick

Woburn

Barton-le-Clay

Harlington

②

A5

B579A

④

Toddington

③

⑨

A6

Leighton
Buzzard

A4012

A5

Luton

①

A505

Houghton
Regis

⑤

Totternhoe

⑦

Dunstable

M1

⑧

B488

B489

⑥ Whipsnade

A5183

Luton and The Chilterns is an area of
striking contrasts – from the gritty bustle
of Luton to the windswept beauty of the
Chiltern Hills. Industry and nature sit
side by side, each shaping the landscape.
For walkers, it offers variety: town trails,
hilltop views and quiet canalside paths.

Luton, the county's largest town, is
known for its vibrant multicultural
heritage, car-making legacy and busy
airport. Dig deeper and you'll find proud
hat-making traditions and historic parks.
Someries Castle, on the edge of town, is
thought to be Bedfordshire's oldest brick
structure – a little-visited reminder of the
area's medieval past.

The landscape rises into the Chilterns,
with sweeping views and chalky ridges
that rival the South Downs. Dunstable
Downs marks the county's highest point,
where gliders drift silently overhead. The
great White Lion carved into the hillside at
Whipsnade is a regional landmark.

Rare flora, including the delicate pasque
flower, thrive here. History is close at hand
too: explore Dunstable Priory or follow the
Grand Union Canal at Leighton Buzzard
for a slower-paced journey. This part of
Bedfordshire has a different energy – more
dramatic and densely populated but no
less rewarding.

Luton and the Chilterns

1 **Leighton Buzzard and the Ouzel Valley** 66
This walk merges canal and street life with riverside and woodland nature

2 **Rushmere Country Park** 68
Enjoy the park's changing seasonal moods with woodland shades, valley views and hidden sculptures

3 **Tebworth and Chalgrave** 70
Discover rural charm and history aplenty in this easily-overlooked corner of the county

4 **Toddington and Sundon Hills** 72
Bedfordshire's hills may come as a surprise on this fine walk that encompasses country villages, gentle farmland and one of the county's highest points

5 **Totternhoe** 74
Explore nature and heritage, where centuries-old landmarks link with diverse habitats and far-reaching views

6 **Whipsnade and Dunstable Downs** 76
You'll soon lose the crowds on this lofty wander with great views

7 **Luton** 78
Saunter through streets shaped by the hatting trade, civic pride and elegant green spaces

8 **East Hyde and Someries** 80
Castle remains and watery habitats meet the urban fringe and the steady hum of jets on this walk

9 **Barton and Pegsdon Hills** 82
This bracing circular walk combines far reaching views with floral riches and tucked-away villages

Leighton Buzzard and the Ouzel Valley

Distance 10km **Time** 2 hours 30
Terrain pavement, towpath, footpath and
water meadows **Map** OS Explorer 192
Access buses to Leighton Buzzard from
Aylesbury, Milton Keynes, Luton and
Dunstable; trains to Leighton Buzzard

**Leighton Buzzard, an elegant town rich in
history and character, offers the perfect
stepping-off point for this stride through
the northern suburbs and out into the
lush River Ouzel valley.**

From the 15th-century Market Cross,
walk along Leighton Buzzard High Street,
where you can admire the lofty spire of
All Saints Church and the Greensand
Ridge Walk sculpture, before turning
right onto Bridge Street. The sculpture
marks the start point of the 64km route
that crosses the county, following the
band of Lower Greensand stone all the
way to Cambridgeshire.

At the roundabout go left and then cross
the zebra crossings and carry on over the
River Ouzel before turning right to follow
the riverside path. Continue ahead for just
over 1km to the Ouzel Meadows (which are
prone to flooding).

Cross the footbridge over the river, then
go left up through the houses, left at
Plantation Road and right up Greenhill –
waymarked 'Ouzel Valley Meander'. At the
crossroads turn left and follow Heath
Road for roughly 750m, passing Heath
Park Drive and then turning left to walk
the length of Heath Park Road. The stone
gatepost is all that's left of the original
entrance to a grand house that once stood
here. Turn left at the T-junction and
continue along the bridleway between the
golf course and Knolls Wood, a remnant of
ornamental planting by local banker John
Dollin Bassett in 1845 which includes an
avenue of Monkey Puzzle trees.

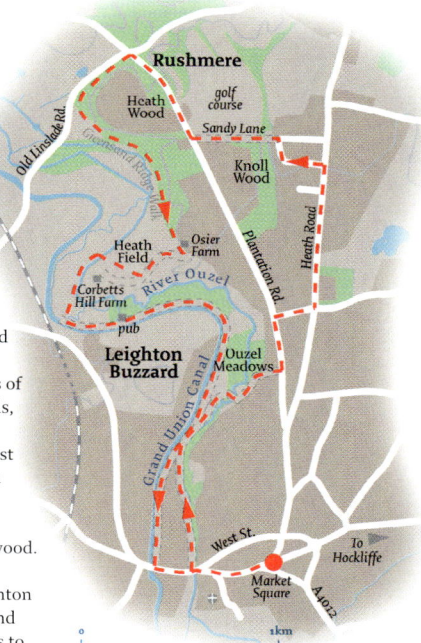

◄ Grand Union Canal

Turn right at the road and soon enter Heath Wood to continue ahead on the downhill path. In the 19th century this was part of the grounds of another long-gone house, The Knolls, and was planted with native and exotic trees – look out for black locust trees, the leaves of which fold up on hot days to save water.

At the crossroads follow the path sharp left to continue through the wood. From here on, the route follows the Greensand Ridge Walk back to Leighton Buzzard. Look across the junction and you'll see the fine old entrance gates to Rushmere Park. Leave the wood to enter Heath Field and turn left to briefly enjoy the open views over the Ouzel Valley. A couple of well-placed benches make for a good pitstop before re-entering the wood and dropping down to follow the path above the broad river meander.

Pass along the back of Osiers Farm, taking a sharp right and walking down the surfaced path. Take the footpath right, cross the bridge and carry on over the water meadows, looking out for heron,

little egret and possibly an otter. This stretch can be very boggy.

Crossing the boardwalk, turn left on joining the towpath of the Grand Union Canal and follow it all the way back to Leighton Road in Leighton Buzzard. This is a lovely stretch with colourful barges, the Globe Inn, Leighton Lock and, if you're lucky, a glimpse of a kingfisher.

At Leighton Road turn left to retrace your steps back to the start point.

Rushmere Country Park

Distance 6km **Time** 2 hours 30
Terrain footpaths and quiet lanes
Map OS Explorer 192 **Access** buses to
Heath and Reach from Milton Keynes
and Aylesbury

Straddling the county boundary with
Buckinghamshire, this walk has a very
different feel to many in this guide thanks
to extensive restoration of heathland and
ancient woodland. A landscape of sandy
soils and interesting habitats supports a
diverse range of fauna and flora, plus
there are views, sculptures and a café to
help make a day of it.

The 400-acre country park is actually a
combination of what were once two
private estates, Stockgrove and Rushmere,
and is now in the care of a partnership
between The Greensand Trust and Central
Bedfordshire Council. The initial 80-acre
Stockgrove site opened to the public in
1972 while the adjacent Rushmere was
added in 2011. The mansion at Stockgrove
was one of the largest country houses built
between the First and Second World Wars.

Start from Stockgrove (not Rushmere)
Visitor Centre. Exiting the car park via
the main entrance, turn immediately right,
go through the kissing gate on the right
and follow the footpath left up the hill,
keeping the fence to your left. Follow this
path through a second kissing gate and
continue to bear left until you reach the
Royal British Legion clubhouse on the edge
of the woods.

Taking a sharp right in front of the
clubhouse continue straight ahead on the
sandy path and follow it across Shire Oak
Heath and Lord's Hill, at times a mass of
bright yellow flowering gorse. Restoration
of this fragile heathland habitat is proving
fruitful, with interesting and rare species
such as green tiger beetle, slow worm
(actually a legless lizard) and adders – our
only venomous snake – now recorded here.

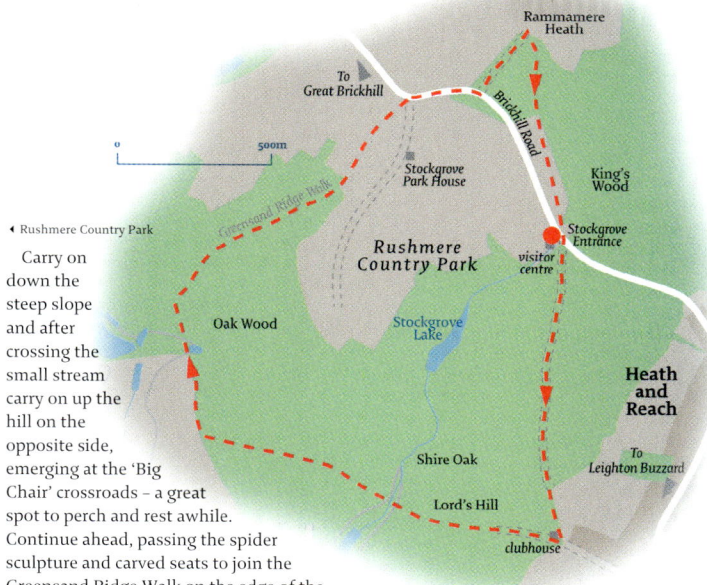

◄ Rushmere Country Park

Carry on down the steep slope and after crossing the small stream carry on up the hill on the opposite side, emerging at the 'Big Chair' crossroads – a great spot to perch and rest awhile. Continue ahead, passing the spider sculpture and carved seats to join the Greensand Ridge Walk on the edge of the woodland. Turn right and follow this path down the hill, enjoying the views over the Buckinghamshire countryside, past the pond and over the bridge.

Continue on the main path, bearing initially to the left (straight ahead is for cyclists only), turn right on the bridleway and walk up the hill through Oak Wood, ignoring a number of paths and continuing ahead on the bridleway. On leaving the wood, pass the row of elegant sandstone cottages on the left and the impressive old watertower of Stockgrove Park House on the right.

Soon emerging onto Brickhill Road, turn right, carefully cross the road and, at the bend with the parking area, turn left onto the bridleway. For the next section there are waymarker posts but they are often a bit overgrown and tricky to follow, so keep to the sandy path to the bottom of the hill, take the right fork and at the path T-junction turn right. Ignore the broad sandy first path on the left but immediately take the next footpath left after this – do not continue ahead uphill on the broad path.

Follow the fenceline through the trees, through a kissing gate and over the meadow back to the start.

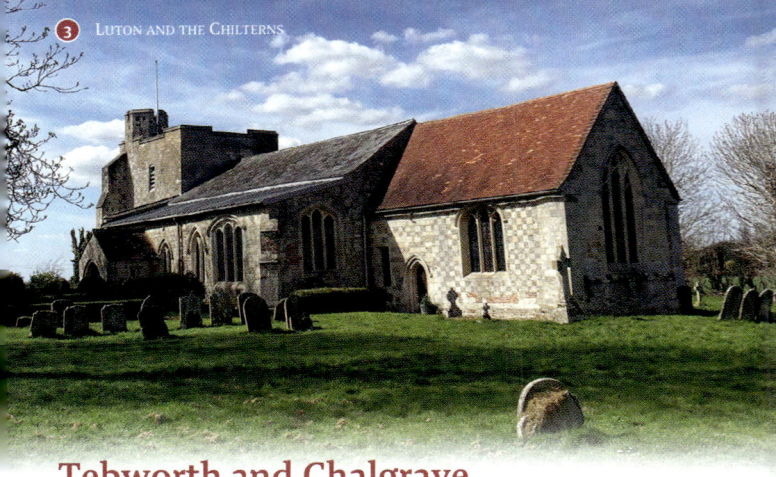

Tebworth and Chalgrave

Distance 11.5km **Time** 3 hours
Terrain footpath, fields and quiet lanes
Map OS Explorer 193 **Access** no public transport to the start; possible to take the bus to Toddington and start at The Glebe

The tiny parish of Chalgrave, which includes the hamlets of Wingfield and Tebworth, is intersected by the Roman road of Watling Street which ran from Dover to Wroxeter, and by the Theedway, a track established by Neolithic travellers long before the Roman conquest and a salt-trading route in Saxon times.

Starting from the centre of Tebworth, with the village sign on your right and Queens Head on your left, proceed along Toddington Road, taking the footpath left just after the pond.

Cross two grazing fields, then turn right along the broad footpath between two hedges. Continuing ahead with the single hedge on your right, keep an eye open for the gate in the hedge and footpath on your right and follow this uphill to the road, in total a distance of around 1.25km. Be aware that in spring these fields are full of ewes with their lambs, so please proceed with caution, particularly if with a dog.

Carefully cross and follow the road verge left for a short distance, then go through the kissing gate and along the permissive path. Follow the hedge past the woodland and around the corner of the field to drop down to The Glebe recreational area on the edge of Toddington.

After crossing the stream go left, then immediately right to follow the hedgeline uphill, then right at the sports pitch. Once through the kissing gate continue ahead over the grassland, crossing first the boardwalk through Dropshort Marsh, a

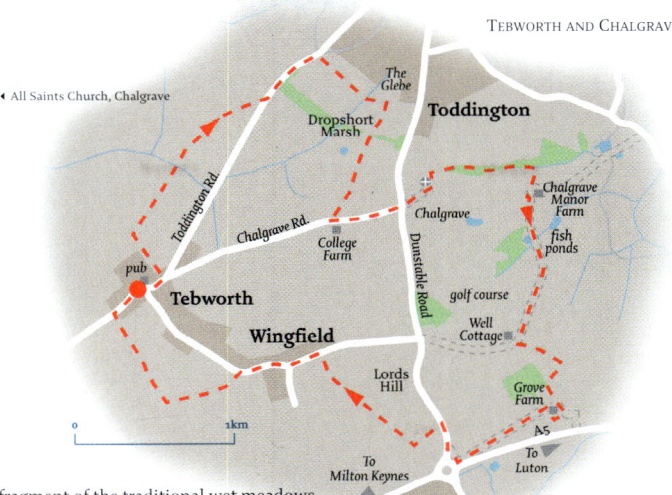

◄ All Saints Church, Chalgrave

fragment of the traditional wet meadows that were once common in this area, and then the field to Chalgrave Road. Go left along the lane for just under 500m, carefully cross the busy Dunstable Road and head down the lane to All Saints Church, with its 13th-century wall paintings rediscovered during works in the 1930s.

Take the bridleway to the right of the church car park entrance and follow it around the graveyard and along the broad hedge-lined track for almost 800m, enjoying the birdsong and butterflies on a warm day. Where the bridleway goes sharp left take the footpath on the right, carefully following the waymarkers around the side of Chalgrave Manor Farm to exit along the main drive. After about 1km pass through the gate at Well Cottage and take the byway on the left, once part of the old Theedway trading route.

Taking the first bridleway on the right, follow the waymarkers around three sides of Grove Farm, then left along the main drive and across the busy B5120 at the traffic lights. Turning right, pass under the pylon and go left along the bridleway, taking the first footpath on the right up into Wingfield. Signs of medieval ridge and furrow farming systems can be seen all around here. Turn left to follow the road through the village and where it bends sharply right cross over and take the stile on the left, then follow the footpath to the right. With views towards the Dunstable Downs and Ivinghoe Beacon, cross three more stiles, then take the footpath on the right and continue ahead up to Hockcliffe Road. Turn right and follow the road into Tebworth and back to the start.

71

Toddington and Sundon Hills

Distance 12km **Time** 3 hours
Terrain footpath, fields, pavements and
quiet lanes **Map** OS Explorer 193
Access buses to Toddington from
Dunstable and Bedford

Running from the west country to East
Anglia, the Icknield Way is made up of
prehistoric pathways and is one of the
oldest roads in Britain. This circular route
forms part of the Icknield Way Trail and
showcases some of the finest scenery in
the heart of Bedfordshire.

From St George Church on the green at
Toddington (on-street parking available),
head down Conger Lane and go left at the
fingerpost. Keep straight ahead through a
couple of gates and then go right past a

run of old Nissen Huts. Keep ahead with
the cemetery on the left and at the bottom
take the left track to go through a gate,
after which turn right and follow the path
downhill for just over 750m.

Cross the road and go through a couple
of gates and over a bridge before
continuing left to cross the service road
over the M1. On the other side of the
bridge, take the left fork and then go right
into a field and follow the track up to the
left. Take the first track on the right and
where it bends sharply right, cross the
field ahead, passing right by the pylon in
the middle. At the far side, go through the
tunnel under the railway.

Immediately after the tunnel, take the
path to the right for almost 500m, then
continue down the right-hand edge of a
field. Go left at a line of trees, keeping the
trees on your right, and at a house follow
the path around the boundary as

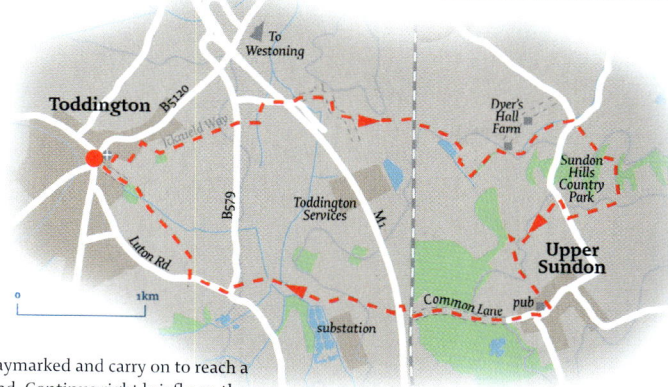

waymarked and carry on to reach a road. Continue right briefly on the road, then pass through a kissing gate, signposted 'Permissive Path', to climb up into Sundon Hills Country Park. Keep climbing up through the woods, going left at a route marker, up some steps, straight on and up more steps. A well-placed bench at the top has a terrific view eastwards to the ancient woodlands on the chalk escarpment of Sharpenhoe Clappers.

From the top of the steps, go right uphill to the top of the field, then right again. At the Sundon Hills car park, take the downhill path parallel to the road, then cross over the road where signposted to continue along the top edge of a field. In the next field, follow the right of way right, downhill, then sharp left to cut past the sewage works to a track, which leads uphill to the Red Lion Pub in Upper Sundon. Go right along the road and then take Common Lane on the right, keeping ahead as it turns into a path before emerging onto a lane. Go downhill here, following the waymarker for a short

stretch of woodland and then crossing the bridge over the railway. At the bottom of the steps, go straight ahead and right up the access ramp to cross over the M1.

On the other side of the motorway, follow the field path up along the northern edge of the substation and round to the left, ignoring the first path off to the right and keeping ahead to cross a bridge over a stream. Keep straight on, heading northwest across the corner of a field to cross another bridge over a stream and then continue northwest across a field (or to the left and around the edge if the field is planted) before taking a bridleway to the left down a line of trees. At the road go left to reach a junction, then right uphill on the pavement for around 300m. Take the signposted path on the right into the field and follow the waymarkers over the fields and up the northern edge of woodland back into Toddington. At the houses, keep straight on to return to the village centre.

◄ Toddington

Totternhoe

Distance 7km **Time** 2 hours
Terrain footpaths and open grassland
Map OS Explorer 192 **Access** buses to
Totternhoe from Dunstable and Aylesbury

Blending the perfect mix of history, wildlife and open landscapes, this walk following old green lanes and byways offers an appealing mix of ancient earthworks, chalk grasslands and peaceful countryside. Keep an eye out for birds of prey soaring above and soak up the stunning views across the valleys and rolling hills.

Totternhoe Knolls, nestled within the Chiltern Hills Area of Outstanding Natural Beauty, is a haven for rare flowers and wildlife and its rich landscape contains numerous orchids and butterflies. The quarry edges, in particular, are the best place in the county to see the rare small blue butterfly.

Leave the car park through the vehicle barrier and head right, making your way uphill along the track. On reaching the T-junction, turn left onto the byway and follow this as it curves right and gently climbs above the village. After about 500m, leave the byway through the kissing gate on the left to explore the Castle Hill earthworks, the remains of an 11th- or 12th-century motte and bailey castle known as Eglemont (Eagle Mount). Little is documented about its origins, but it offers a fine 360-degree view.

In spring, violets emerge in this area and early butterflies like brimstone and comma seek out warm sheltered spots. Migrant warblers and skylarks bring summer alive with their song. Throughout the year, keep watch for birds of prey – kestrel, buzzard and red kite – patrolling the skies.

Descend from the trig point atop the

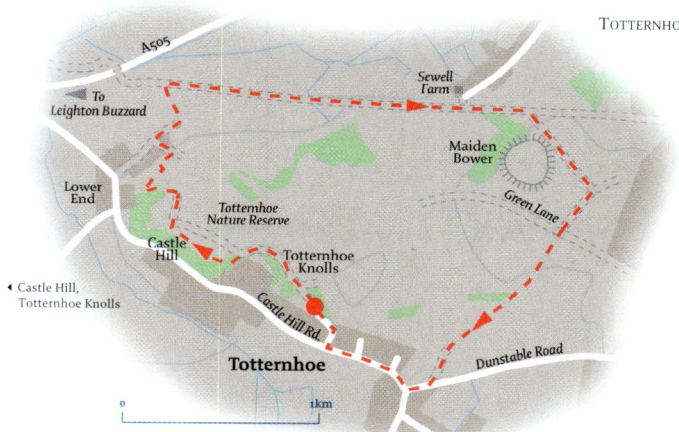

Castle Hill,
Totternhoe Knolls

motte, go through the kissing gate and turn immediately right, on through another gate, then left to rejoin the byway dropping downhill. Just before the houses turn right at the waymarker post and keep on down to the road. Cross over the works entrance and continue along the byway, turning left at the T-junction along the bridleway to join the Sewell Greenway. This is a shared path following the course of the former railway that ran between Leighton Buzzard and Dunstable.

Turn right onto the Sewell Greenway and follow this for 1.8km. To your right lies the chalk quarry, a site shaped by centuries of excavation. The local stone, known as clunch, has long been prized for its fine quality, especially in ornamental stonework. Its legacy can be seen in some of the nation's grandest architecture – including Westminster Abbey and Windsor Castle.

Just after the bridge bear right, leaving the Sewell Greenway, to climb uphill along a bridleway. Either fork right to explore Maiden Bower, keeping left to rejoin the bridleway, or stay with the bridleway, which makes a sharp right turn with views of Maiden Bower to your right. Although Maiden Bower doesn't look like much more than a circular hedge today, it actually marks the boundary of an Iron Age fort.

Ahead is the edge of Dunstable. After the sharp right turn on the bridleway, continue ahead, through the crossroads with Green Lane, to drop back down to Totternhoe village, with fine views as you go. The area is crossed by many green lanes, old drove roads along which livestock would have been taken to and from Dunstable.

At Dunstable Road, turn right and when it becomes Castle Hill Road take the third turning on the right for a final climb and return to the start.

Whipsnade and Dunstable Downs

Distance 7km **Time** 2 hours 30
Terrain footpaths, grassland and fields
Map OS Explorer 182 **Access** no public
transport to the start, but buses from
Dunstable to Whipsnade and Kensworth

This walk takes in Bedfordshire's highest
point on the Downs, as well as Whipsnade
village and the unique Tree Cathedral.
Rolling hills and steep escarpments, fine
views over four counties and, on the
ground, rare habitats combine in an
exhilarating jaunt.

Starting from the Chilterns Gateway
Centre car park, head downhill past the
centre to the sculptural windcatcher which
ventilates the centre. From here, turn left
at the waymarker post onto the bridleway,
which runs beside the hedgerow and
woodland and is part of the Icknield Way
Trail. There are expansive views across the
vale. Follow the path for 1.3km as it
contours around the hillside, looking out

for a glimpse of the Whipsnade White
Lion, carved in the ground in 1933 as an
advertisement for the zoo and a warning
to low-flying pilots to avoid disturbing the
animals. During the Second World War it
was covered with a tarpaulin to prevent it
being used for navigation from the air.

The Downs are sculpted and eroded
from chalk that first formed at the bottom
of a warm shallow sea approximately 70
million years ago. Chalk grassland,
traditionally managed by flocks of sheep,
is a rare habitat rich in biodiversity,
including the county flower, the bee
orchid and the scarce Duke of Burgundy
butterfly. Pass through the gate and,
leaving the valley view behind, follow the
fingerpost for the Tree Cathedral along the
bridleway through a tunnel of trees – once
a medieval route between Whipsnade and
Eaton Bray to the north.

After the house turn left and continue to
the remarkable Whipsnade Tree Cathedral.

76

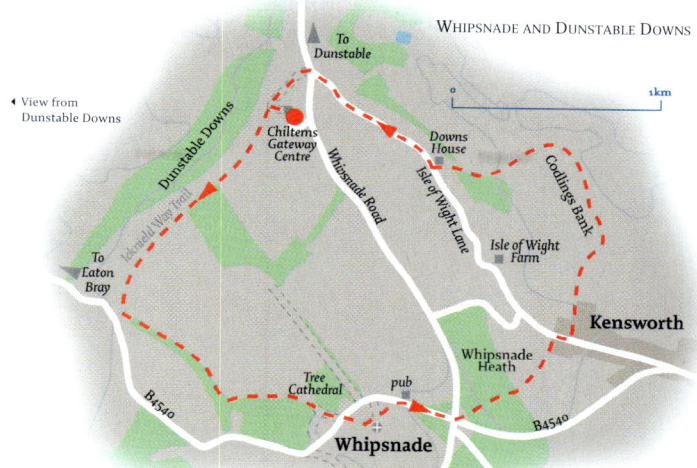

◄ View from Dunstable Downs

The idea was conceived by Edmund Kell Blyth, an officer with the Oxfordshire and Buckinghamshire Light Infantry, as a memorial to three friends from the First World War, combining the beauty of nature and majesty of a cathedral. Planting began in 1930 and includes a porch of mighty oaks, nave of lime and semicircular chancel of silver birch.

Continue into Whipsnade, most famous for its zoo, but the lesser visited village itself has an attractive setting around a large green. Turn left to pass the church, with its unusual dedication to St Mary Magdalene, and carry on carefully along the road at the thatched Old Hunters Lodge pub to the roundabout. Proceed straight across, then head immediately left into Whipsnade Heath, once an area of open heath but since the decline of sheep grazing now colonised by trees and scrub. Take the woodland footpath straight ahead through the heath, along a field edge and onwards to emerge on the edge of Kensworth village.

Turn right at the road and then quickly left at the footpath fingerpost, soon leaving the farm and industrial units behind and heading downhill into the undulating countryside. Pass the rusting barn, continue on up the gradual slope and turn immediately left when entering the wood. Upon exiting veer right to follow the footpath along the field edge, keeping the hedge to your left, and at the waymarker post go left on the footpath through another woodland and along the edge of a field.

At Downs House turn right to follow Isle of Wight Lane along to the Robertson Corner Memorial, carefully cross Whipsnade Road and turn left to return to the Chilterns Gateway Centre.

Luton

Distance 4km **Time** 1 hour
Terrain pavements and town parks
Map OS Explorer 193 **Access** buses to Luton
from Bedford, Dunstable, Hitchin,
Leighton Buzzard and Milton Keynes;
trains to Luton from Bedford and London

**This short urban amble around Luton
seamlessly mixes both past and present,
offering opportunities to enjoy the sights
and sounds of its modern-day cultural
vibes whilst dipping a toe into its proud
hatting history. Even the football club is
fondly known as 'The Hatters'.**

From the main Luton train station
head away from the town centre, taking
the High Town exit, cross the road, turn
left and then right to walk up High Town
Road. Continue along High Town Road,
passing the Victorian methodist church
hall and galleried church. Turn left onto

Havelock Road at The Painters Arms, a
long-standing Luton institution.

Carry on for around 500m to the end of
Havelock Road, passing St Matthews
Church, along Bell's Close Park, then up a
slight incline to Pope's Meadow. Along
with a connecting wood, these green areas
are jointly known as People's Park and
were gifted in the 1860s by the Midland
Railway as compensation for their
building works in the town.

The top of Pope's Meadow has a great
view and, unsurprisingly, this is a popular
sledging hill in winter. Head diagonally
left down the hill and cross over Old
Bedford Road into Wardown Park through
the pillared entrance. Follow the path
along to the right, keeping to the outer
routes to reach the museum at Wardown
House via the tennis courts, bowls greens,
East Lodge and Summerhouse. Dating

from 1877, the house has been home to the town museum since 1931 and includes a permanent hatting exhibition and café. On leaving, walk diagonally left down to the boating lake, passing the bathing hut and continuing along to the bandstand, suspension bridge (don't cross), boathouse (boats for hire during the warmer months) and along to the drinking fountain. Cross the bridge here and go around to the left to rejoin Old Bedford Road.

Cross the road and turn right to head back to High Town, staying on Old Bedford Road for around 750m. From Clarendon Road onwards this area had more of a 'cottage' hat industry, where small producers worked from modest workshops attached to their homes. The hat-making industry started in the late 1600s but boomed in the 19th century, as the Napoleonic Wars blocked imports, while the arrival of the railway in 1858 supercharged production. During its Victorian heyday a third of Luton's population was involved.

Continuing along Old Bedford Road look out for no 86, Ken Peirson and Son, who still manufacture women's hats, the narrow Frederick Street Passage and Mussons Path that served as rear service roads for the hat workshops.

At the mini-roundabout go left onto North Street, then curve right on Dudley Street. Many of the larger surrounding buildings on the approach to Midland Road were once hat factories or warehouses. Turn left at Midland Road to return to the start.

▸ Wardown Park, Luton

East Hyde and Someries

Distance 12km **Time** 3 hours
Terrain cyclepath, footpaths, pavements and lanes **Maps** OS Explorer 193 and 182
Access buses to Luton Airport Parkway from Luton; trains to Luton Airport Parkway from Bedford and London

Urban and pastoral collide on the edges of Luton in a walk that, unusually, includes a section adjacent to the airport runway. In the late 18th century this was the seat of the 3rd Earl of Bute, Prime Minister to George III, who lived at stately Luton Hoo.

Leaving Luton Airport Parkway, cross the car park, picking up the blue Upper Lea Valley Way waymarker arrow which directs you left. Pass the multi-storey car park and, just before the roundabout, go left onto the traffic-free Luton to Harpenden route, following the line of the old Hatfield, Luton and Dunstable railway. The first third of this walk (just over 4km) follows the Upper Lea Valley Way, initially parallel to busy roads and flyovers, but it soon swaps the urban fringes for a more rural scene along the River Lea and views to the right to the grounds of Luton Hoo, designed in the 18th century by Capability Brown. Along the way the path climbs gently up to a bench and sculpture celebrating local heroes, including comedian Eric Morecambe, who made his home in Harpenden.

Stay on the main Valley Way, keeping to the left at the path junction, taking the longer route to Someries Castle. Pass the sewage works and, at the road junction, continue ahead – the private house here was once Luton Hoo Station. At the next road junction turn left to East Hyde, crossing the River Lea. The route goes right and immediately left onto Far's Lane, but take a brief detour left to visit St Charalambos Greek Orthodox Church. Head up Far's Lane and just after the

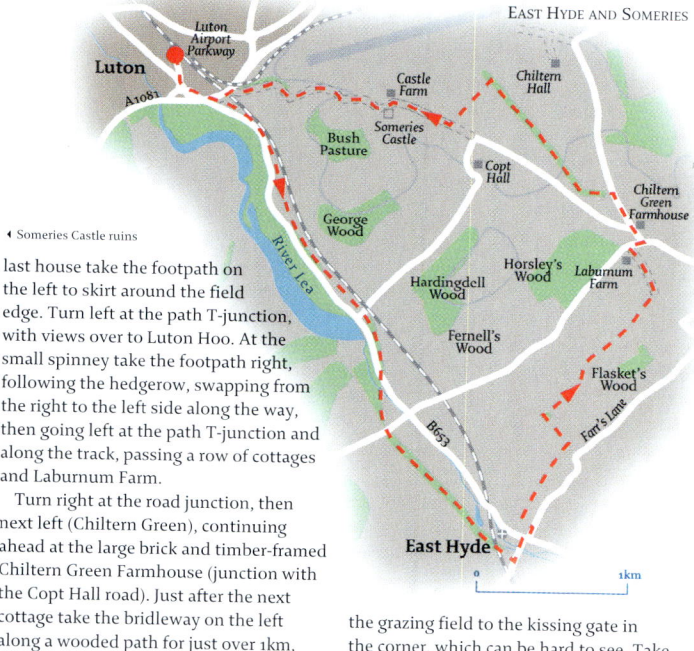

◄ Someries Castle ruins

last house take the footpath on the left to skirt around the field edge. Turn left at the path T-junction, with views over to Luton Hoo. At the small spinney take the footpath right, following the hedgerow, swapping from the right to the left side along the way, then going left at the path T-junction and along the track, passing a row of cottages and Laburnum Farm.

Turn right at the road junction, then next left (Chiltern Green), continuing ahead at the large brick and timber-framed Chiltern Green Farmhouse (junction with the Copt Hall road). Just after the next cottage take the bridleway on the left along a wooded path for just over 1km, keeping ahead at the path junction and soon exiting the wood along the field edge to a farm track (can be overgrown).

Turn right and continue to the gatehouse and chapel ruins of 15th-century Someries Castle, more of a fortified manor house than a castle, largely built by Lord John Wenlock, Chamberlain to Henry VI's wife, Queen Margaret of Anjou. This is the oldest brick building in the county and one of the earliest surviving in England.

Continue through the adjacent kissing gate and take the path diagonally across the grazing field to the kissing gate in the corner, which can be hard to see. Take the footpath to the right, along the field edge and downhill, following the Luton airport boundary.

Go hard right to stay with the perimeter fence, taking the path through the woodland, then right on exiting the wood, right at the footpath waymarker and down the steps to rejoin the web of busy roads and DART (Direct Air-Rail Transit) shuttle. Follow the road left for approximately 100m before dropping down to rejoin the Valley Way outbound route and turn right to return to Luton Airport Parkway station.

Barton and Pegsdon Hills

Distance 14km **Time** 3 hours 30
Map OS Explorer 193 **Access** buses to
Barton-le-Clay from Bedford, Luton and
Milton Keynes

A walk of quiet splendour spanning two
counties, two nature reserves and an
ancient roadway, climbing from expansive
valley bottoms to downland slopes with
some of the county's most arresting views.
Start at St Nicholas Church, Barton-le-
Clay, noted for its 15th-century
chequerboard tower. Follow Church Road
south to its end and turn left onto the
bridleway. Pass through the kissing gate
and begin the steady climb into Barton
Hills National Nature Reserve. Looking
back for a fine view, Barton lies tucked
beneath the northern Chilterns, le-Clay
referring to the village's location on a
ridge of sticky gault clay soil, a
characteristic feature where the chalky
Chilterns begin to slope.

Stay on the main path, climbing onto
the escarpment and along its top, with
views all around. Barton Hills is a classic
chalk downland; look out for orchids,
pasque flowers and scabious in spring and
summer, alongside butterflies such as
chalkhill blues and dark green fritillaries.
This stretch feels more like the South
Downs than the heart of Bedfordshire.
After about 850m, take a sharp right and
exit the reserve via two kissing gates. Turn
left to follow the field edge, continuing
ahead on a broad track over farmland. At
the road, turn left for 150m, then right
onto a bridleway. Continue ahead under
the pylon, then turn left at the track
crossroads by the wood.

This next section follows the Icknield
Way Trail northeast for around 3km. After
around 1km, at the road, follow the road

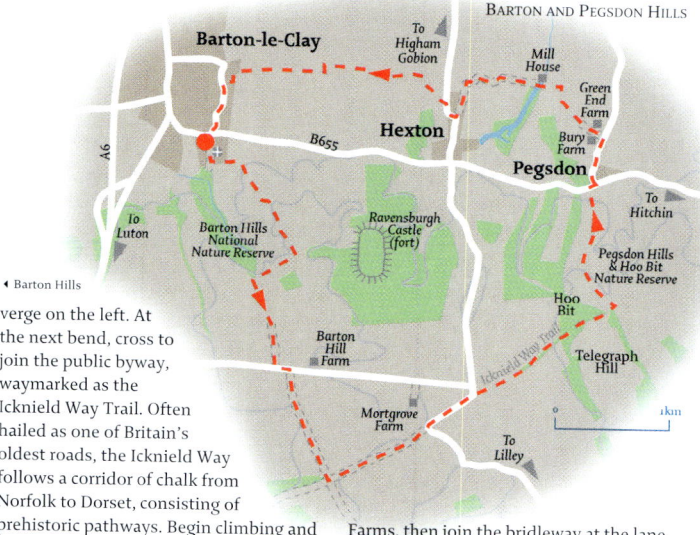

◄ Barton Hills

verge on the left. At the next bend, cross to join the public byway, waymarked as the Icknield Way Trail. Often hailed as one of Britain's oldest roads, the Icknield Way follows a corridor of chalk from Norfolk to Dorset, consisting of prehistoric pathways. Begin climbing and at the waymarker post stay ahead on the byway through a fine beechwood, skirting Telegraph Hill. At the Wildlife Trust's Pegsdon Hills information board, go left into the reserve. Keep ahead on the clear path for just over 1km – but first nip right to take in the expansive view.

This is one of the jewels of the Chilterns – steep chalk slopes with sweeping views and rich wildlife year-round. Spring brings grizzled skippers; in summer, look for the eerie green glow of glow-worms; while winter offers charms of finches feeding in the hedgerows. Descend from the escarpment to reach the hamlet of Pegsdon. Cross the busy road and continue ahead. At the T-junction turn left and follow the verge for 400m. Take the dead-end lane left, passing Bury and Green End

Farms, then join the bridleway at the lane end. At the fingerpost take the left-hand bridleway, pass Mill House and follow Mill Lane as it winds toward Hexton.

You're now in Hertfordshire. At the junction, turn right towards Higham Gobion – but first continue ahead to explore charming Hexton with its popular pub and curios shop. Backtrack and continue past the recreation ground, shortly after this taking the footpath diagonally left across the field (signed Barton). Cross the bridge and follow the hedgerow, keeping to the field edge. Stay on this track back to Barton-le-Clay, eventually crossing a stream and passing behind houses. At the road turn left, following Manor Road down to Hexton Road, at which go right and then left down Church Road to return to the start.

Greensand Ridge, near Ampthill ◄

Greensand Ridge Walk

The Greensand Ridge is a distinctive geological feature running across central Bedfordshire – a raised band of sandstone formed millions of years ago from ancient river and coastal deposits. Unlike the adjacent chalky Chilterns, the warm iron-rich Greensand lends the landscape a softer character and russet tint to local buildings. Churches built from it offer clear glimpses of the ridge's geology in everyday architecture.

Stretching for around 64km, this long-distance walk weaves through a rich cross-section of the county's landscapes and history. Starting near Leighton Buzzard, it passes canals, heathland, farmland and river valleys, linking grand estates and historic villages. Highlights include Woburn, Ampthill, Old Warden and Sandy, before finishing

generally easy to follow. and green discs, the route is throughout with fingerposts Well waymarked sight in the wild. these escapes are now a familiar Woburn Park in the early 20th century – muntjac deer, a species introduced to The route's waymarker logo features a Rushmere Country Park. Great Park and the woodlands of can enjoy sweeping views from Ampthill Cambridgeshire. Along the way, walkers just over the county boundary in

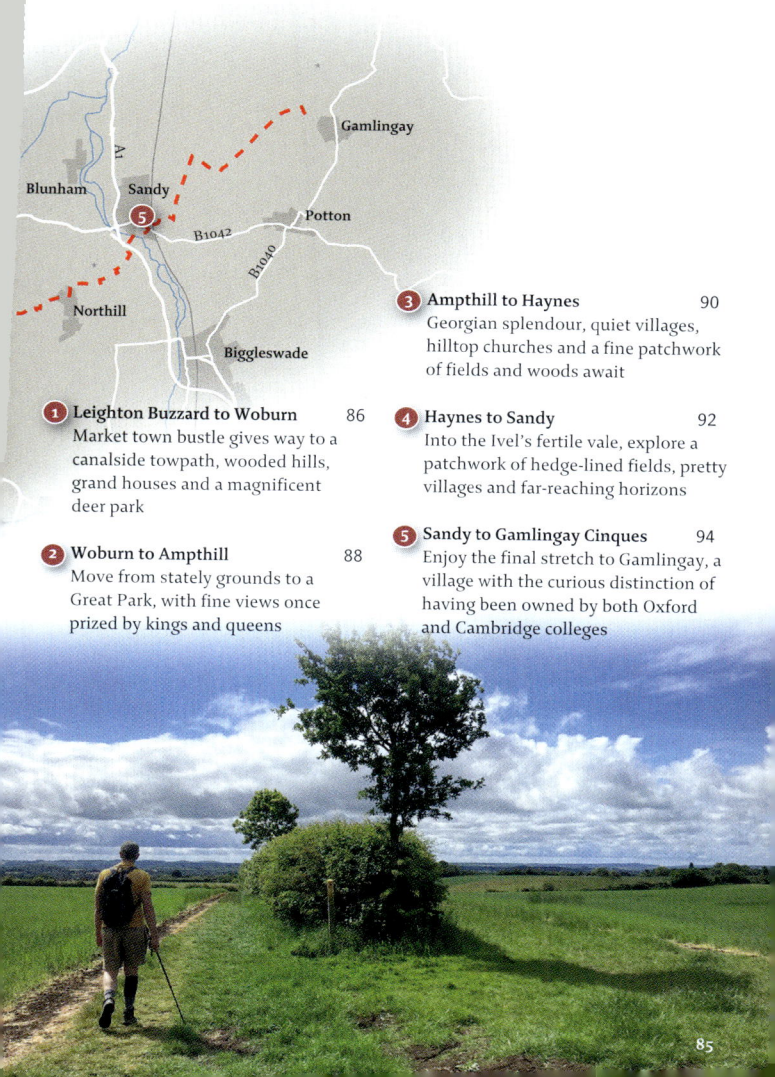

Gamlingay

Blunham   Sandy

⑤

A1

B1042

Potton

B1040

Northill

Biggleswade

① **Leighton Buzzard to Woburn**   86
Market town bustle gives way to a
canalside towpath, wooded hills,
grand houses and a magnificent
deer park

② **Woburn to Ampthill**   88
Move from stately grounds to a
Great Park, with fine views once
prized by kings and queens

③ **Ampthill to Haynes**   90
Georgian splendour, quiet villages,
hilltop churches and a fine patchwork
of fields and woods await

④ **Haynes to Sandy**   92
Into the Ivel's fertile vale, explore a
patchwork of hedge-lined fields, pretty
villages and far-reaching horizons

⑤ **Sandy to Gamlingay Cinques**   94
Enjoy the final stretch to Gamlingay, a
village with the curious distinction of
having been owned by both Oxford
and Cambridge colleges

Leighton Buzzard to Woburn

Distance 14km **Time** 3 hours 30
Terrain footpath, towpath, farmland and
pasture **Map** OS Explorer 192 **Access** buses
to Leighton Buzzard from Aylesbury,
Milton Keynes and Luton; trains to
Leighton Buzzard

This first section of the Greensand Ridge
Walk offers a fairly gentle introduction to
the route with a unique mix of landscapes
not seen elsewhere in the county.
Beginning from Leighton Buzzard's
graceful High Street, the route follows the
Grand Union Canal, before ascending the
Greensand Ridge to pass over heathland,
then finishing in elegant Woburn.

From the Greensand Ridge sculpture on
Leighton Buzzard High Street, follow
Bridge Street to the roundabout, go left
past the Fly Past sculpture and cross the
zebra crossing, then continue along
Leighton Road for 25om. At the Grand
Union Canal turn right to follow the

towpath for approximately 2km. Just after
the Globe Inn turn right through a kissing
gate, go along the boardwalk and into the
water meadow of the River Ouzel. Follow
the waymarkers through this boggy
section, cross the river bridge and turn left
uphill, then sharp left at the houses.

Pass Osiers Farm, walking with the
wood to the right and valley to the left for
700m, then take the short steep path to
emerge into a meadow. Continue along
the wood edge, then go right onto the
woodland path leading to Rushmere
Park's old gates. Cross the road and turn
left at Bragenham Lane, then right into
Rushmere Country Park. Walk along the
old driveway, passing the giant sequoias,

the tallest trees in the county.

At the end of the open grassland take the left path into the woods. Though there are no waymarkers at this point, they soon reappear. Follow them through the woods for roughly 2.3km, past a pond and over the bridge, bearing initially to the left. Turn right on the bridleway up the hill through Oak Wood and, passing a number of paths, continue ahead on the bridleway. On leaving the wood, walk past handsome sandstone cottages to the left and the old watertower of Stockgrove Park House to the right.

Emerge onto Brickhill Road, turn right and at the bend with the parking area go left onto the downhill bridleway, veering left to head around the western edge of Rammamere Heath. Exit onto and cross a grazing field towards Rammamere Farm. Don't go through the gate; instead turn right and follow the fenceline. Go through the next gate, up to the wood, and then turn left over a stile and footbridge into another field. King's Wood on the right has the largest population of lily-of-the-valley in the county.

Go over a boggy stretch and cross the busy A5 road. Walk up the other side and across the fields to Sheep Lane, at which turn left for 150m and then left again onto the grass ride. Carry on ahead through an area of young trees, enter a wood and at the waymarker turn right to follow the path full

of white blackthorn blossom in spring. Pass the thatched cottage at Job's Farm, turn left just before the road along the field edge, cross the road and continue along the pavement for 400m. Just before the Woburn sign, cross to the footpath and go through a kissing gate, up the field and then along the edge of Wayn Close, a broad riding with views of Woburn Abbey ahead. Before you reach the road, go left and exit onto George Street, completing this section.

Woburn to Ampthill

Distance 18.5km **Time** 5 hours
Terrain footpaths, parkland and fields
Maps OS Explorer 192 and 193
Access buses to Woburn from Leighton
Buzzard, Dunstable and Milton Keynes

**With some of the finest views along the
Greensand Ridge Walk, this stage leads
through a landscape rich in history and
natural beauty. Enjoy picturesque
villages, historic estates and serene
parkland and keep an eye open for soaring
red kites, brimstone butterflies in spring
and skylarks in summer. In autumn you
may hear the echo of rutting deer.**

From the car park on Park Street in
Woburn, turn left and left again at the
crossroads. Pass the fire station, where the
first Greensand Ridge Walk stage joins
from the right. At Ivy Lodge turn left
through the metal gate into the Deer Park,
following the waymarked path straight
across the parkland for around 2km,
passing Woburn Abbey and exiting via the
large gate. Continue along the waymarked
path through the woods, across a field,
then past Linden Lake and onto the road.

Turn left into the picturesque village of
Eversholt – composed of some 13 'Ends,'
including a Witts End. Pass St John's
Church and at the cricket field turn right
into Brook End, passing the cottages. Cross
a bridge to the left, then go immediately
right to follow the field boundaries.
Continue left onto the bridleway and
follow this to New Water End. Cross the
road and take the track opposite, shortly
passing through woodland and along a
field edge, past Wakes End Farm and
across Cobblers Lane.

Cross the sandy field and continue
around the northern edge of the

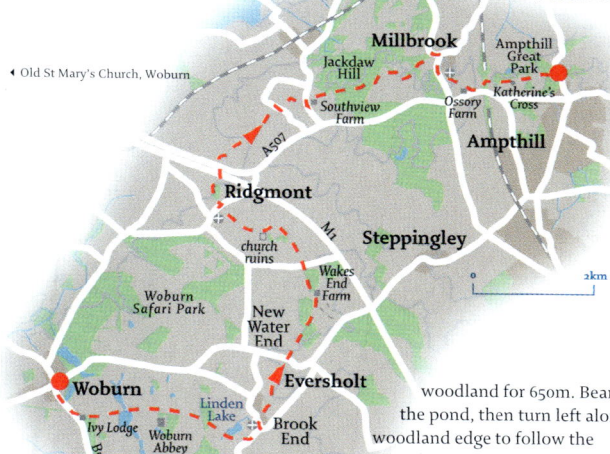

◄ Old St Mary's Church, Woburn

woodland, then turn left at the far end to the ruins of Segenhoe Church, with its bench and information boards. Cross the fields to Ridgmont, turning right along the main street, then take the lane downhill to the left, just before the Rose & Crown pub. At the end of the woodland, turn right, then take the path left over a field and cross the M1 and Ridgmont Bypass. Follow the field boundaries for around 1.4km to Boughton End and turn right onto the lane, then left uphill after approximately 100m. At the copse of trees, take the path on the right across the field to the next road junction.

Turn left along the road and then quickly right onto a track at Southview Farm. After passing Jackdaw Hill House follow the waymarked route through the woodland for 650m. Bear right at the pond, then turn left along the woodland edge to follow the waymarked path between the golf course and Millbrook Proving Ground.

At the road, turn right and head up to Millbrook village. Turn right again along Sandhill Close, then left onto an uphill path just after the Old Village Hall. Pass St Michael's Church, perched overlooking the vale. Bear right and continue along the farm track, passing Ossory Farm, and follow the metal fence. Turn right to walk up steps through the woodland into Ampthill Great Park, which since the 15th century has served as a royal residence, hunting ground and landscaped garden.

Continue straight ahead up onto the escarpment, joining the gravel path, to pass Katherine's Cross and enjoy fine views towards Bedford. Where the straight gravel path veers right, continue ahead on the grassy path, past numerous benches, and on through the wood to complete this section at Bedford Street (B530).

Ampthill to Haynes

Distance 14km **Time** 3 hours 30
Terrain footpaths, fields and quiet lanes
Maps OS Explorer 193 and 208
Access buses to Ampthill from Bedford
and Milton Keynes

Ampthill, a gracious Georgian market
town with a fascinating history, marks the
start of this section of the Greensand
Ridge Walk, which also runs past striking
ruins and across rolling countryside.
Woodland, farmland and rare sandy acid
grassland shape a varied landscape,
scattered with picturesque villages and
sandstone churches.

From the town pump in Ampthill, head
along Bedford Street, passing the
supermarket and climbing the hill. At the
top cross the road carefully and follow the
lane towards Houghton House ruins,
thought to be John Bunyan's House
Beautiful from *The Pilgrim's Progress*. Turn

right just after the houses and follow the
track behind the barns to the southern
corner of King's Wood, at which go
through the right-hand kissing gate, then
right to descend along field boundaries
and grassland tracks to Kings Farm on the
edge of Maulden.

Cross straight over at The Brache and
continue down to the village. Turn left
onto George Street for approximately
260m, then take a left along the
waymarked path by Woodcocks Cottage,
leading to St Mary the Virgin Church.
The Ailesbury Mausoleum, built by the 1st
Earl of Elgin, was one of England's first,
and the church interior features fine
Sgraffito plasterwork.

Go through the churchyard, then left
through the car park and across Church
Meadow SSSI. At the first kissing gate
follow the waymarked route along the
edge of Maulden Wood, taking a quick left-

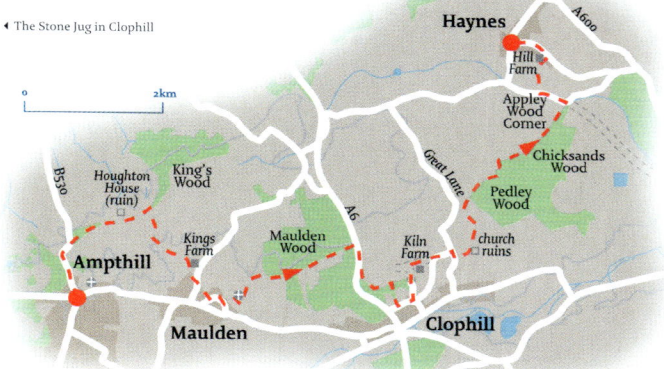

◀ The Stone Jug in Clophill

right at the track with the thatched cottage.

At the curve in the track with the waymarker, the official Greensand Ridge Walk turns left into woodland, then immediately right to wind along an often-overgrown woodland path, following tricky-to-spot waymarkers.

Alternatively, stay on the track (this route is still marked on OS maps), curving right, then left at Clayhill Cottages, where both options soon merge.

Carefully cross the A6 dual carriageway, then follow the verge downhill before turning left after the stone banking and up the steps into woodland. Continue along the field edge and turn right, then left around two sides of a paddock, before going briefly downhill; turn right at the wooden fence end, soon emerging on Back Street in Clophill. Turn left and continue for 250m past the Stone Jug pub, then take a left into The Slade. At the last house, bear right into the wood, through a

smallholding, then up to Old Kiln Lane, turning right past Kiln Farm.

At the T-junction, go left onto Kiln Lane, then right at Great Lane. At the fingerpost, take the footpath left up to a track running in front of St Mary's Old Church ruins. Follow the track around the churchyard, then along the waymarked footpath, passing through numerous kissing gates.

Cross the footbridge and turn immediately right along the field edge beside Pedley Wood. This soon merges into Chicksands Wood, from which oak timbers were used in the construction of Ely Cathedral. Here, you can either enter the wood, turning left to follow a woodland path, or stay on the outer edge – both routes lead to Appley Wood Corner.

Turn left along the road for about 430m, then turn right onto the bridleway, going over fields and through Hill Farm to the road. Turn left here for Haynes village centre and the end of this section.

Haynes to Sandy

Distance 13.5km (or 16km with seasonal route change) **Time** 3-4 hours
Terrain footpaths, pavements and quiet lanes **Map** OS Explorer 208
Access buses to Haynes from Bedford, Shefford and Hitchin

This section of the Greensand Ridge Walk offers varied scenery and glimpses into centuries of rural and monastic history, with sweeping views across both the Great Ouse and Ivel river valleys.

From Haynes village hall head left along Northwood End Road and take the Greensand Ridge Walk-waymarked footpath on the left, bearing right across the field to reach the busy A600 at Deadman's Cross. Here, between 2 March and 31 October, you can take a shorter route via a permissive path. With care, cross the A600 heading left. Take the permissive path on your right along a broad cinder track through Warden Great and Little Woods. Cross the road to follow the Greensand Ridge Walk fingerpost along the wide bridleway track.

From 1 November to 1 March, the only option for this section is on minor roads. Turn right along the pavement for around 800m to reach the crossroads at Rowney Warren Wood. Carefully cross and take the lane signed 'Old Warden' for around 850m, ignoring the first right but taking the next lane on the left. Follow this for around 2.5km to the T-junction at Abbey Farm – location of a once great Cistercian abbey. Turn left along the busier road for almost 750m, then right to follow the fingerpost along the wide bridleway track.

Look left for a panoramic view over the Great Ouse valley, Bedford and the Cardington Hangars, today used for film and concert sets. Continue past the Wildlife Trust's Old Warden railway tunnel reserve (worth a short loop). Where the track curves sharp right, keep ahead on

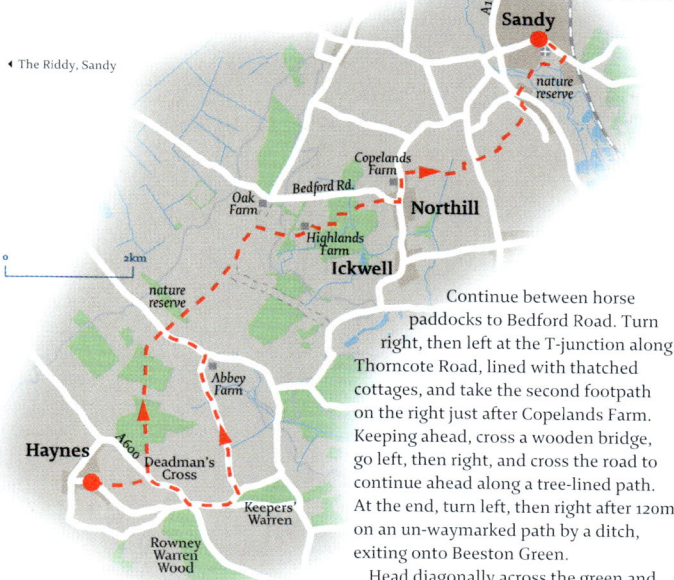

The Riddy, Sandy ◄

HAYNES TO SANDY

Continue between horse paddocks to Bedford Road. Turn right, then left at the T-junction along Thorncote Road, lined with thatched cottages, and take the second footpath on the right just after Copelands Farm. Keeping ahead, cross a wooden bridge, go left, then right, and cross the road to continue ahead along a tree-lined path. At the end, turn left, then right after 120m on an un-waymarked path by a ditch, exiting onto Beeston Green.

Head diagonally across the green and take The Crescent on the right. Go through an alleyway and cross the A1 via the footbridge, then head north along the pavement (against the traffic flow) and turn right into The Baulk. Pass the chapel and the road narrows to a hedged path, crossing the River Ivel at The Riddy – a wildlife-rich remnant of once widespread flood meadows.

Turn right at the weir and follow the surfaced path, crossing the river again after approximately 450m. Continue along Ivel Road to Sandy High Street. The next stage continues ahead, but to end this leg turn left past St Swithun's Church into Sandy town centre.

the path to the right of the hedgerow. This stretch can be muddy. After two fields, the path curves right, crosses a small bridge and then continues left along a wide yew tree-lined track.

Take the second footpath on the right. Pass between fields, through a tree belt and across a paddock around the distinctive Georgian farmhouse of Highlands Farm. Go through the kissing gate and small wood, along the field edge path and into Home Wood, bearing left, then right at the Greensand Ridge Walk signs. Exit via a kissing gate just after the sign for the medieval fishponds, stocked to feed the Lords of Northill Manor.

93

Sandy to Gamlingay Cinques

Distance 9km **Time** 2 hours
Terrain pavements, field tracks and paths,
quiet lanes **Map** OS Explorer 208
Access bus to Sandy from Biggleswade;
trains to Sandy from London and
Peterborough. For the return trip, bus to
Biggleswade or Sandy from Gamlingay

Taking its name from the low range of
sandy hills on the eastern side of town,
Sandy was once an important Roman
trading centre and staging post, and an
Iron Age hillfort overlooking the town
and the valley of the River Ivel is known
locally as 'Caesar's Camp'. To the north
lies RAF Tempsford, from where supplies
and agents were dropped into occupied
Europe during the Second World War.
Brave Violette Szabo, whose story is told
in the film *Carve Her Name with Pride*, flew
her first mission from here in April 1944.

From the car park at Belfry Court, exit
to the High Street and turn left, shortly
after going left again up St Swithun's Way.
(The previous section of the Greensand
Ridge route joins here from Ivel Road on
the other side of the High Street.)

Go right along Stonecroft and then left
as waymarked up the left-hand side of a
block of garages. Cross the main East
Coast railway over the bridge and
continue straight ahead up the meadow,
gradually bearing left to climb up steps cut
into the hill. At the top go immediately
right and on reaching a fence continue to
the left, dropping down to Sand Lane.

Continue to the right to reach a junction
after 500m, at which take the waymarked
bridleway to the left. Follow this for 2.25km,
crossing over or alongside six fields in total,
following the route of a Roman road.
Look out for kestrel and red kites here

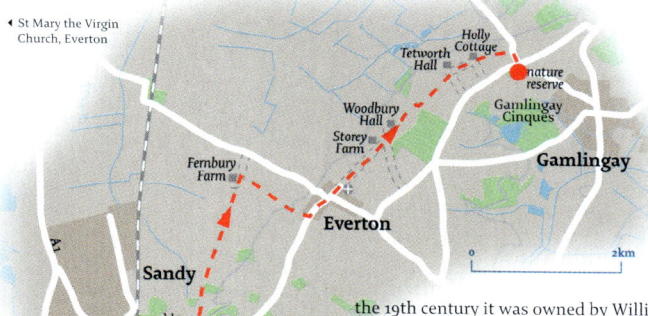

◀ St Mary the Virgin
Church, Everton

and note that livestock may be grazing.

At Fernbury Farm, keep ahead on the track, then take the waymarked path to the right along a field edge and up a short steep climb to the village of Everton. A handy bench is positioned at the top of the hill, a good spot to enjoy the view back down over the Ivel valley.

Go left into Everton and where the road bends to the right at the Thornton Arms pub continue ahead on Church Road, passing a pretty row of cottages on the left, then the 12th-century St Mary's Church on the right. At the gate to Woodbury Hall and Storey Farm keep ahead up the drive, carrying on past the farm buildings and then across parkland (cattle may be grazing). Woodbury Hall was one of several country houses originally built in the early 18th century along the top of the Greensand Ridge. In

the 19th century it was owned by William Booth, of the Booth's gin family. At the end of the drive, where it bends left, keep ahead to go through a gate, across a field and through another gate.

Continue right and then left as waymarked across the Tetworth Estate on a signposted obvious route, enjoying the view of Tetworth Hall to the left, built in 1710 in Queen Anne style.

Carry on along a driveway and where it bends right at Holly Cottage continue ahead along a grassy track. At the end go right along the road to a junction, cross carefully and continue ahead into the village of Gamlingay Cinques (pronounced *sinks*). The unusual name is thought to derive from the soft marshy ground – 'sinks' – once typical of this area.

The walk ends in the Wildlife Trust's nature reserve car park on the right, from where it's a 10-minute walk into nearby Gamlingay on the border with Cambridgeshire. To reach the village centre, continue down Cinques Road from the car park and turn right at the end along Waresley Road.

Index

Ampthill — 36, 88, 90
Aspley Guise — 28
Barton-le-Clay — 82
Bedford — 8
Biggleswade — 52
Blunham — 50
Campton — 60
Clophill — 90
Cockayne Hatley — 54
Cople — 46
Dunstable Downs — 76
East Hyde — 80
Eversholt — 32, 88
Everton — 94
Felmersham — 16
Flitton Moor — 38
Flitwick — 38
Gamlingay — 94
Great Barford — 50
Great Ouse, River — 8, 10, 12, 14, 16, 18, 46, 50, 66
Harrold — 14
Haynes — 90, 92
Heath and Reach — 68, 86
Henlow — 58
Hexton — 82
Higham Gobion — 42
Husborne Crawley — 28
Ickwell — 48, 92
Ivel, River — 56
Kensworth — 76
Keysoe — 24
Langford — 58
Leighton Buzzard — 66, 86
Lidlington — 34
Luton — 78
Marston Moretaine — 34
Maulden — 90
Melchbourne — 22
Meppershall — 62
Millbrook — 88
Milton Bryan — 32
Northill — 48, 92
Oakley — 10
Odell — 14
Old Warden — 48
Pavenham — 10
Pegsdon — 82
Potton — 52
Radwell — 16, 18
Rushmere — 66, 68, 86
Sandy — 92, 94
Sandy Heath — 52
Sharnbrook — 18
Sharpenhoe — 40
Shefford — 60
Shelton — 22
Shillington — 62
Silsoe — 42
Someries — 80
Stevington — 10
Stotfold Mill — 56
Sundon Hills — 40
Sutton — 52
Tebworth — 70
Tempsford — 50
Thurleigh — 20
Toddington — 70, 72
Totternhoe — 74
Turvey — 12
Upper Dean — 22
Upper Gravenhurst — 62
Upper Sundon — 72
Whipsnade — 76
Willington — 46
Wingfield — 70
Woburn — 30, 86, 88
Wrestlingworth — 54
Yeldon — 22